FOUNDATIONS

Building a Solid Christian Life

BY
DR. GIL STIEGLITZ

PTLB
PRINCIPLES
TO LIVE BY
LIFE IS RELATIONSHIPS

FOUNDATIONS: BUILDING A SOLID CHRISTIAN LIFE

Copyright © Gil Stieglitz 2016

Published by Principles To Live By, Roseville CA 95661. All rights reserved.
For more information about this book and the author, visit www.ptlb.com

ISBN 978-0-9968855-1-5
RELIGION/Christian Ministry/Discipleship

Cover Design by John Chase
Copyedited by Jennifer Edwards @ jedwardsediting.net
Book Design by Linńe Garrett @ 829design.com

All Scripture verses are from the New American Standard Bible unless
otherwise indicated.
New American Standard Bible: 1995 update.
1995 La Habra, CA: The Lockman Foundation.

Printed in the United States of America

Contents

Introduction

Her name is Diana. She is highly educated and curious about Christianity. I knew her because she was a part of a new Christian's class at the church where I worked. This was the place where people came with their questions and a desire to learn about their spiritual journey toward God and Jesus Christ. Diana had never really cared about God, church, or Jesus before, but now, curiously, she did. I explained to the class that God sends out a call to people to be in relationship with Him.

When a person responds to that call, their sense of being drawn toward Him gets stronger. She said to those in her group, "That is what is happening to me!" She went on to explain how she had not been interested in God before but now she needed to check out this whole "Jesus thing." She made sure that they understood she was not yet a Christian, but she was following this drawing toward Jesus by attending the class. Those of us in the class were witnessing first hand how God was drawing Diana into relationship with Him. We reassured her that as she responded to His love, power, and forgiveness, He would give her more light to continue moving forward towards Him.

Another couple across the table shared a similar story. "That is exactly what happened to us. We thought we were going crazy! We came out of our old religion and have found a completely different interaction with God through Jesus. We knew God was drawing us towards Jesus and a few weeks ago we became Christians. Having a relationship with God is really different, like a going back and forth with God instead of just following a set of rules."

The Bible says, "Today, if you hear his voice, do not harden your hearts." (Ps. 95:7-8; Heb. 4:7) I have the privilege of talking with all kinds of people who are being drawn toward faith. Naturally they have a lot of questions. This material helps answer many of the most basic questions about living in dynamic connection with God. It is important to explain the Christian life to people who are experiencing it, as well as for those who are curious about God and Jesus.

This book is a basic starter in what it means to live the Christian life and to interact with God through Jesus Christ. If you have been a Christian for a long time, or you are just taking a look at the Christian life, jump in and let's build a solid foundation for right thinking about faith.

Welcome

Thank you for choosing to move forward with learning about the Christian faith. This book and the class that goes with it will explain the crucial, foundational building blocks for your life as a Christian. You may be reading this book for a number of reasons:

1. You feel drawn toward God and you're not sure what Christianity is all about.

2. You may have just started attending a new church;

3. You may have begun asking God for help and you want to know more;

4. You prayed a prayer at the end of a service and you were directed to this class;

5. You may have recently asked Jesus Christ to become your Savior and Lord;

6. It has been awhile since you went to church or interacted with God, and you want to understand how to reconnect with Him.

I recommend that you read all of this material as a whole, as each section is like a block that builds upon another. Skipping over or missing one may be detrimental to your growth and enjoyment of the Christian life and your experience with your church. Like the foundation of a building, missing one block upsets the whole structure.

Our goal is to help you build a strong foundation of Christian truths so that your spiritual house will be strong enough to withstand the storms and rocky paths of life. (MATT. 7:24-26; LUKE 15:28-30)

Building Block #1: Jesus Christ and the Christian Life

In this first chapter, we will help you understand more about what it means to be a Christian and about Jesus. This is an exciting set of materials that will help you understand how to build a great foundation for your Christian life. We will explore ten truths about God and show you what happens as a person begins to live their Christian life. We discuss what happens when a person first becomes a Christian and why some people might have doubts that God accepts and loves them after they have made a decision to become a Christian. We also share over thirty promises from God that are realized when a person becomes a Christian.

Building Block #2: Growing as a Follower of Christ

In this second chapter, we discuss how a Christian learns to follow Christ and the benefits that come from being a disciple. The entirety of the Christian path is laid out in an easy to understand way. We discuss baptism and all that it means as one of the first steps in the normal Christian life, and how to keep our relationship with Jesus Christ alive so that our relationship with God stays vital and powerful. We learn about the ten major relationships and the ten major truths that form Christian living and Christian thinking. And we provide answers to the ten basic questions of life and how Christianity answers these questions.

Building Block #3: The Wonder of the Church

The Church is a wonderful creation of God. Many people do not understand how vital and important the church really is. In this third week of materials, we will discuss what the church is and why it is so important. Because the church has failed in many cases to live up to what it is supposed to be, individual Christians and the society at large have either turned away from church completely or have not engaged with it in a way that was intended. Because of this, they have been robbed of God's blessings that were supposed to come through the church. We will discuss the nine vital actions that only the church can take and what happens when it does what it is supposed to. We will also explore how a few different churches have put these principles into practice within their churches.

Building Block #4: Finding and Living in the Will of God

All Christians desire to live in the will of God. Christians seem to instinctively know that if they are in the center of the will of God, then they will have a life of meaning, purpose, significance, and love. However many are not experiencing the wonder of God's will because they do not understand three crucial things. In this chapter, we explain three aspects of finding and enjoying God's will—the process of making wise decisions; filling our lives with His love in various ways; and understanding and deploying our unique combination of gifts, dreams, abilities, and experiences, so that we can see how we are to make a unique contribution to the people and the world around us.

Building a foundation for our Christian lives is important.

It requires time and attention to the materials in this class and book, but it will be worth it. ISAIAH 55:10-12 promises us that any time or effort we spend learning about God and His Word is the most profitable thing we can do:

"As the rain and the snow

come down from heaven,

and do not return to it

without watering the earth

and making it bud and flourish,

so that it yields seed for the sower and bread for the eater,

so is my word that goes out from my mouth:

It will not return to me empty,

but will accomplish what I desire

and achieve the purpose for which I sent it.

You will go out in joy

and be led forth in peace;"

My hope is that you will allow God to lead you on this journey of faith and toward a life of joy and peace. May your spiritual foundation become strong so that you can do all God has for you here.

FOUNDATIONS

BUILDING BLOCK #1

Jesus Christ and the Christian Life

Building Block #1
Jesus Christ and the Christian Life

Who Is Jesus Christ?

A common thought that people have is, "If there is a God, why hasn't He communicated with us?" Actually He has in a number of ways. God tells us in the Bible that He has communicated with us through the Creation, through the still, small voice in our spirit and conscience, through the Bible and the fulfillment of its prophecies and power, through various signs and wonders, through preachers and teachers, and most importantly, through His own Son, Jesus Christ. God tells us about Himself and what He is like through all of these ways, but the clearest communication about Him is Jesus Christ, who He sent to live among us as a human in order to show us what He is really like. Look at what Scripture says about Jesus:

HEBREWS 1:1-3

God, after He spoke long ago to the fathers in the prophets in many portions and in many ways, in these last days has spoken to us in His Son, whom He appointed heir of all things, through whom also He made the world. And He is the radiance of His glory and the exact representation of His nature, and upholds all things by the word of His power. When He had made purification of sins, He sat down at the right hand of the Majesty on high,

Jesus Christ is a big deal. He is the first foundational block, the cornerstone, and the key to the Christian life. Understanding Him fully and completely is critical to your faith in Him. Whatever church you attend, it is vital that Jesus is made central to everything that is done or said because He is the bedrock. Otherwise, the church is built on the beliefs of men and will ultimately fail. We believe that embracing Jesus Christ as God and Savior is the most important thing anyone can do for their lives. Faith in Jesus allows everything else in life to make sense. It brings everything in life into its proper order and with the correct perspective. Let me help you understand why Jesus Christ is central.

Twelve Key Truths about Jesus Christ

The Bible communicates twelve truths about who Jesus is and what He accomplished during His time on Earth.

1. **We understand and believe that Jesus was, is, and forever will be God. He was God before time began and will be God when time ends.**

    JOHN 1:1-3,14

    In the beginning was the Word, and the Word was with God, and the Word was God. He was in the beginning with God. All things came into being by Him, and apart from Him nothing came into being that has come into being. And the Word became flesh, and dwelt among us, and we beheld His glory, glory as of the only begotten from the Father, full of grace and truth.

REVELATION 1:17,18

And when I saw Him, I fell at His feet as a dead man. And He laid His right hand upon me, saying, Do not be afraid; I am the first and the last, and the living One; and I was dead, and behold, I am alive forevermore, and I have the keys of death and of Hades.

Notice that in the above verses from various parts of the Bible, Jesus is clearly called God and displays Himself as God. Jesus was God before the world began and He will be God after the world ends. One of the most important revelations about God that comes from the Christian faith is that God is a triune God. We call this concept "The Trinity," which consists of "The Father," "The Son," and "The Holy Spirit."

2. **We understand and believe that Jesus took on human nature and a human body through the normal birthing process. He became a man approximately 2,000 years ago in order to become humanity's Savior. He made a way for us to reconnect with God through His life, death, and resurrection.**

LUKE 2:6-11

And it came about that while they (Joseph and Mary) were there, the days were completed for her to give birth. And she gave birth to her first-born son; and she wrapped Him in cloths, and laid Him in a manger, because there was no room for them in the inn. And in the same region there were some shepherds staying out in the fields, and keeping watch over their flock by night. And an angel of the Lord suddenly stood before them, and the glory of the Lord shone around them; and they were terribly frightened. And the angel said to them, "Do not be afraid; for behold, I bring you good news of a great joy which shall be for all the people; for today in the city of David there has been born for you a Savior, who is Christ the Lord."

PHILIPPIANS 2:5-10

Have this attitude in yourselves, which was also in Christ Jesus, who, although He existed in the form of God, did not regard equality with God a thing to be grasped, but emptied Himself, taking the form of a bond-servant, and being made in the likeness of men. And being found in appearance as a man, He humbled Himself by becoming obedient to the point of death, even death on a cross. Therefore also God highly exalted Him, and bestowed on Him the name which is above every name, that at the name of Jesus every knee should bow, of those who are in heaven, and on earth, and under the earth,

Notice in the above verses that Jesus was fully human at the same time that He was fully God. He was willing to be a servant and lay aside the independent use of His divine nature and in that way become our Savior. It is because He is a human that He can be our Savior. It is important to realize that Jesus really was both God and man. He lived His human life dependent on the Father and the Holy Spirit just as a human should. Because Jesus was a human, he could truly take away our sins and become our representative.

3. **We understand and believe that He lived a perfect, sinless life.**

HEBREWS 4:14,15

Since then we have a great high priest who has passed through the heavens, Jesus the Son of God, let us hold fast our confession. For we do not have a high priest who cannot sympathize with our weaknesses, but One who has been tempted in all things as we are, yet without sin.

Notice in the above verses that Jesus lived His life without sinning. He lived his whole human life and did not violate God's laws or His leading. He faced the highest level of temptations, but he never gave in. Because He successfully lived a human life without sin, He can sympathize with our weaknesses. He is qualified to be our high priest; that is, our direct gateway to God.

4. **We understand that Jesus voluntarily gave up what His perfect life earned, so that we could have an opportunity to enjoy relationship with God.**

JOHN 10:17,18

For this reason the Father loves Me, because I lay down My life so that I may take it again. No one has taken it away from Me, but I lay it down on My own initiative. I have authority to lay it down, and I have authority to take it up again. This commandment I received from My Father.

2 Corinthians 5:21

*He made Him who knew no sin to be sin on our behalf,
so that we might become the righteousness of God in Him.*

Notice that in the above verses Jesus is the reason that God can love us and forgive us. Without the sacrifice of Jesus, we would have no hope of having a relationship with God.

5. **We understand and believe that He died on a cross approximately 2,000 years ago.**

Matthew 27:50-54

And Jesus cried out again with a loud voice, and yielded up His spirit. And behold, the veil of the temple was torn in two from top to bottom; and the earth shook and the rocks were split. The tombs were opened, and many bodies of the saints who had fallen asleep were raised; and coming out of the tombs after His resurrection they entered the holy city and appeared to many. Now the centurion, and those who were with him keeping guard over Jesus, when they saw the earthquake and the things that were happening, became very frightened and said, "Truly this was the Son of God!"

Jesus' death on the cross was an actual historical event that had huge, spiritual significance. At just the right moment of history, God entered the world in Jesus Christ and showed us what He was like. Jesus, the God-man, lived a perfect life and then was willing to give up His life to pave the way back to the Father. God the Father heaped the sins of all mankind upon the sinless Son of God, who gave up his perfect life to pay for those sins.

6. We understand and believe that Jesus was resurrected from the dead after three days.

MATTHEW 28:1-10

Now after the Sabbath, as it began to dawn toward the first day of the week, Mary Magdalene and the other Mary came to look at the grave. And behold, a severe earthquake had occurred, for an angel of the Lord descended from heaven and came and rolled away the stone and sat upon it. And his appearance was like lightning and his clothing as white as snow. The guards shook for fear of him and became like dead men. The angel said to the women, "Do not be afraid; for I know that you are looking for Jesus who has been crucified. He is not here, for He has risen, just as He said. Come, see the place where He was lying. Go quickly and tell His disciples that He has risen from the dead; and behold, He is going ahead of you into Galilee, there you will see Him; behold, I have told you." And they left the tomb quickly with fear and great joy and ran to report it to His disciples. And behold, Jesus met them and greeted them. And they came up and took hold of His feet and worshiped Him. Then Jesus said to them, "Do not be afraid; go and take word to My brethren to leave for Galilee, and there they will see Me."

2 CORINTHIANS 5:17-19

Therefore if anyone is in Christ, he is a new creature; the old things passed away; behold, new things have come. Now all these things are from God, who reconciled us to Himself through Christ and gave us the ministry of reconciliation, namely, that God was in Christ reconciling the world to Himself, not counting their trespasses against them, and He has committed to us the word of reconciliation.

The true story of the resurrection of Jesus changes everything. It means that God was in Jesus reconciling the world to Himself. Notice that because of what Jesus did through His death and resurrection, God is no longer holding people's sins against them. God has opened a way to be in relationship with Him even though we are not perfect. God raised Jesus up from the dead because His work of redemption was accomplished.

7. **We understand and believe that Jesus ascended into Heaven.**

   ### ACTS 1:9

   And after He had said these things, He was lifted up while they were looking on, and a cloud received Him out of their sight.

Notice that the story of Jesus does not end with the resurrection, but He returns to Heaven after forty days of appearances and teaching to His most loyal followers. The fact that Jesus went to Heaven after the resurrection gives us assurance that He is there now, carrying on ministry for us and waiting to return.

8. **We understand and believe that Jesus is currently in Heaven praying for us.**

HEBREWS 4:16

Let us then approach God's throne of grace with confidence, so that we may receive mercy and find grace to help us in our time of need.

HEBREWS 7:24,25

But Jesus, on the other hand, because He continues forever, holds His priesthood permanently. Therefore He is able also to save forever those who draw near to God through Him, since He always lives to make intercession for them.

One of the things that Jesus is doing in Heaven is making requests to God the Father on behalf of the believers. When we pray to Jesus, He will listen and act on our behalf. We can ask Jesus for anything, however our requests should not be selfish, but should be according to God's will. We should ask for lots of things to happen, like things that can change us or other people. This allow us to fulfill His commands to us.

9. **We understand and believe that Jesus will come back again to wrap up history.**

MATTHEW 24:30

And then the sign of the Son of Man will appear in the sky, and then all the tribes of the earth will mourn, and they will see the Son of Man coming on the clouds of the sky with power and great glory.

Notice that there is a day when Jesus Christ will return to Earth to wrap up history, as we know it. For thousands of years now, Christians have been anticipating Christ's return. There are certain events that need to take place before He will return. Whenever the last event happens, He will come. One thing that has to happen is for the last person to enter into fellowship with Jesus Christ through faith in this age. There are other signs that Jesus gives us in Matthew 24. One thing is for sure—there will be no doubt in anyone's mind when He finally does return; He will be seen and heard by everyone.

10. We believe that Jesus is still alive.

1 THESSALONIANS 1:9,10

For they themselves report about us what kind of a reception we had with you, and how you turned to God from idols to serve a living and true God, and to wait for His Son from heaven, whom He raised from the dead, that is Jesus, who rescues us from the wrath to come.

All of the other religions of the world have founders who died. Their followers worship at their graves or shrines dedicated to them. Christians understand that their founder rose from the dead and is alive forever more. He does not have a grave where people can make pilgrimages. He is as close as a prayer.

11. We understand and believe that Jesus sent the Holy Spirit back to dwell in, guide, and minister to each person who accepts Him as their Savior and Lord.

JOHN 16:7,13,14

But I tell you the truth, it is to your advantage that I go away; for if I do not go away, the Helper will not come to you; but if I go, I will send Him to you. But when He, the Spirit of truth, comes, He will guide you into all the truth; for He will not speak on His own initiative, but whatever He hears, He will speak; and He will disclose to you what is to come. He will glorify Me, for He will take of Mine and will disclose it to you.

One of the greatest gifts that Jesus gave us is the gift of the Holy Spirit. Jesus, the man, could only be in one spot, and only so many people could interact with Him. Jesus tells us that it will be better when He goes to Heaven, because He will send back the Holy Spirit who can have a personal and interactive relationship with each believer.

12. **We understand and believe that anyone who has faith in Jesus as their Savior and Lord will be forgiven of their sins and given a right relationship with God along with many other blessings.**

JOHN 1:12

But as many as received Him, to them He gave the right to become children of God, even to those who believe in His name.

JOHN 3:16

For God so loved the world that He gave His only begotten Son, that whoever believes in Him shall not perish, but have eternal life.

2 Corinthians 5:17-19

Therefore if anyone is in Christ, he is a new creature; the old things passed away; behold, new things have come. Now all these things are from God, who reconciled us to Himself through Christ and gave us the ministry of reconciliation, namely, that God was in Christ reconciling the world to Himself, not counting their trespasses against them, and He has committed to us the word of reconciliation.

We invite you to do further research about the life and teaching of Jesus. We invite you to learn more about Jesus by reading or listening to the gospel accounts of His life: Matthew, Mark, Luke, and John. There have also been a number of helpful books (beyond the gospel accounts) that have been written about Him.

Here are a few we recommend:

More Than a Carpenter	by Josh McDowell
Who Moved the Stone?	by Frank Morrison
Delighting in Jesus	by Gil Stieglitz
This Changes Everything	by Ray Johnston

God invites you to trust Jesus Christ as your payment for sins. He wants you to let Him direct your life. There are many ways to live your life and there are many things you can depend upon for the next life. But God invites you to depend only upon Him and what He did in and through His Son Jesus Christ. Jesus is the way into the good graces of God Almighty. Jesus said, "I am the way, the truth, and the life. No one comes to the Father except through Me." (JOHN 14:6)

Confessing Christ as Lord and Savior

When a person asks Jesus Christ to be their Savior and Lord, this is what makes them a Christian. This confession is the culmination of a process that began before they prayed the prayer and will continue into eternity. The decision to become a Christian activates many new processes. It is this prayer to invite Jesus Christ to become your Savior and your Lord that changes everything. For one thing, we are asking God to change us, to forgive us, and to develop us into the person He knows we can be.

Reconnection with God

For some people, this book and the class that goes with it represents a time when they are reconnecting with God after a time away from following Him. They were close to God in the past, but have drifted away from Him over the years. Now they want to come back to a connected relationship. God promises that when we become Christians, we become His adopted sons and daughters. (ROM. 8:12-17) Like our own children, we can rebel and go our own way, do our own things, but it doesn't disqualify us from His love. He will never leave us or forsake us, and nothing can separate us from His love. (ROM. 8:31-39) He doesn't let us go easily. He pursues us and woos us back into relationship with Him, patiently waiting until we find our way. (JOHN 6:44) The process of reconnecting with God is often just like the process of connecting for the first time. It can oftentimes be a very emotional process as we realize what we have done. Praying a simple prayer asking for forgiveness, admitting that we did many selfish and sinful things, and renewing the commitment to allow Jesus Christ to be our Savior and Lord is all that is required. We ask Jesus to come into our lives and transform us into the kind of person He wants us to be.

The Process of Salvation

The process of salvation begins with drawing and ends in final consummation. Let's look at the diagram below and see how Scripture says this amazing blessing occurs.

Foundations Class 1

Your new life in Christ:

How does becoming a Christian happen?

What is the process of salvation?

Drawing	Awareness	Convinction	Salvation	Assurance	Transformation	Consummation
Christ	Christ	Christ	Christ	Christ	Christ	Christ You
					You Christ	
				You Christ		
You	You	You	You			
John 6:44	John 1:29	Rom 3:10 Rom 3:23 Rom 6:23	John 1:12 John 3:16 2 Cor 5:17	1 John 5:13 Rom 8:16	Phil 1:6; 2:12-14 Rom 12:2; 8:29 John 14:17	1 John 3:2

Where would you say you are on this diagram?

Drawing:

God calls out to people to establish a relationship with Him so that we will be forgiven, healed, and directed to the best life.

JOHN 6:44

No one can come to Me, unless the Father who sent Me draws him; and I will raise him up on the last day.

Notice that we do not seek after God but He seeks after us. His drawing, calling, and/or urging to reconnect with Him includes the power to respond. Theologians tell us that we did not have the power to seek or respond until He began seeking us. But then in His drawing of us, He provides the power to respond.

Awareness:

At some point, we become aware that this strange urge to connect with God is from God Himself, and that He wants a relationship with us through His Son, Jesus Christ. We become aware of Jesus Christ, who He is, and what He can do for us.

JOHN 1:29

The next day he saw Jesus coming to him, and said, "Behold, the Lamb of God who takes away the sin of the world!"

Notice that in this verse, the people who had seen Jesus before finally realized who He was, and they really wanted to know more about

Him. God makes it clear where and who to seek.

Conviction:

There will come the realization at some point that we are guilty before a holy God and have nothing to offer Him to earn a relationship with Him. We have a need and there is nothing we can do about fixing it. Only God can fix this problem.

> ### ROMANS 3:10
>
> *As it is written: There is none righteous, not even one;*

> ### ROMANS 3:23
>
> *For all have sinned and fall short of the glory of God,*

> ### ROMANS 6:23
>
> *For the wages of sin is death, but the free gift of God is eternal life in Christ Jesus our Lord.*

Notice that we become aware of our need for God and this brings us to another level of our searching for God. We realize that we are disconnected because of our sin and selfishness, and we begin to understand that we cannot solve the problem that gets in the way of our desired relationship with God. This is not a problem that we can fix. We are not prepared in ourselves to connect to God, but we desperately want to have a relationship with Him. It is important to feel and know that this is a problem that we cannot solve. The solution must come from God. And delightfully, it has come in Jesus the Christ, the Son of God, who was born into this world, lived a perfect life, and then voluntarily gave up His life to give us the solution to our dilemma. That is the Good News!

Belief Resulting in Salvation:

We become aware that all God is asking for is faith (belief) in Jesus Christ as our Savior. God gives forgiveness, restoration, and the hope of Heaven as free gifts. God has done all the work for us. All we have to do is embrace Jesus Christ as our payment for sin (Savior) and as the new boss (Lord) of our life.

> ### JOHN 1:12
>
> *But as many as received Him, to them He gave the right to become children of God, even to those who believe in His name.*

> ### JOHN 3:16
>
> *For God so loved the world that He gave His only begotten Son, that whoever believes in Him should not perish, but have eternal life.*

> ### 2 CORINTHIANS 5:17
>
> *Therefore if any man is in Christ, he is a new creature; the old things passed away; behold, new things have come.*

Notice that God does all the work. We just have to receive the work of Jesus Christ into our lives. We do not do anything in reconnecting to God; God does it all. We receive the work of God into our lives through faith or belief. God gives us the solution to the problem that we cannot fix, which is wrapped inside faith in Jesus Christ as our Savior.

Think of it this way. Salvation is like God, who asks us to take a pill that will change us in order to have a relationship with Him. When we trust Him and decide to take the pill, we will be given:

- Forgiveness;
- Right relationship with Him;
- Connection to God's guidance;
- New desires toward love and righteousness;
- Abilities to help others we did not have before;
- Ability to love our enemies;
- Citizenship in Heaven;
- New truth about our world, what to worry about, and what to let go of.

This pill is Jesus the Christ, the Savior and Lord of the World. We take the pill by believing in Him as our only hope for connection with God and all the other benefits. We put our full faith and trust in the work of Jesus Christ in our life as we accept Him as our Savior and Lord. This requires belief and a full surrender to God's plan for salvation.

There have been some who have faked taking the pill in order to look good to other Christians, or to get something they wanted. But these folks always become known over time because they do not change into more loving, Christ-like people. The power to change into a loving, God-connected person comes from Jesus Christ inside us, not from us in our own power.

When we call out to Jesus the Christ and ask Him to be our Savior, He will begin the work of empowering us for a life that is beyond anything we could do on our own. He begins to change us into the kind of person He wants us to be one step at a time. It is a wonderful privilege to sense God's call and then respond with a full surrender to Him.

Assurance:

After we have prayed a prayer of belief in Jesus Christ, He fills our heart with assurance that we have taken hold of the eternal life. We are children of God.

1 JOHN 5:13

These things I have written to you who believe in the name of the Son of God, in order that you may know that you have eternal life.

ROMANS 8:16

The Spirit Himself bears witness with our spirit that we are children of God.

Notice that it is possible to know whether you have really taken Jesus Christ in to your heart and that He is working in your life as your Savior. He gives us assurance that He is working in us, and that we have His eternal life working in us. He is forgiving us and changing us into His image, shaping us for deep relationship with Him and Heaven.

Yes, it is possible to resist what God is doing in us, and in this way, we grieve the Holy Spirit, who operates within us. We will all do this from time to time but that does not stop His urging and work in us. Resisting Him just causes us to miss some of the wonders that He has planned for us and causes us to continue to receive the consequences of our selfish and self-directed life.

If you have truly believed in Jesus the Christ as your Savior and Lord, then you begin to notice Him urging, prompting, and working on you to cooperate with Him in the life-change process He is doing in, on, and for you.

Some people believed in Jesus at an early age or stage of their life, but they now need to bring their faith of the past into their present, believing in Christ at their current mental, emotional, physical, and spiritual place. Some call this a "rededication" or "recommitment" to Jesus Christ. Whatever it is called, it signals to God that you intend to cooperate with the process that He wants for you and in you.

If you sense no work of God in your life, or you have no desire to connect with God or to make progress in becoming a more loving, righteous fit for Heaven, then you may have been faking your belief or were insincere in your belief at some earlier stage in your life.

I would suggest that you pray a prayer of faith and ask Jesus Christ into your life as your Savior and your Lord. Begin the process now. I have seen a number of people who have said:

> *"Okay Lord, if I didn't do it right before or for some reason it didn't work at that time, I do surrender my life now to Jesus Christ as my Savior and as my Lord. I do want you in my life, running it and making me the kind of person you want me to be. I realize that I cannot do this on my own. I need you and want you guiding, directing, and saving me."*

Transformation:

After we become Christians, God works with us to grow in our Christian lives by helping us understand ten spiritual realities and how Jesus wants us to live in the ten major relationships of our life.

PHILIPPIANS 1:6

For I am confident of this very thing, that He who began a good work in you will perfect it until the day of Christ Jesus.

PHILIPPIANS 2:12-14

So then, my beloved, just as you have always obeyed, not as in my presence only, but now much more in my absence, work out your salvation with fear and trembling; for it is God who is at work in you, both to will and to work for His good pleasure. Do all things without grumbling or disputing.

ROMANS 12:2

And do not be conformed to this world, but be transformed by the renewing of your mind, that you may prove what the will of God is, that which is good and acceptable and perfect.

ROMANS 8:29

For whom He foreknew, He also predestined to become conformed to the image of His Son, that He might be the first-born among many brethren.

JOHN 14:17

That is the Spirit of truth, whom the world cannot receive, because it does not behold Him or know Him, but you know Him because He abides with you, and will be in you.

Notice that God will be active in your life in many ways and at different times in order to transform you into the loving, righteous, and joyous person He has in mind. Becoming a Christian is not a fire insurance policy, but it is a life-change contract with God to work in you in order to bring out a newer, better, and more grounded person—one who is not as distracted by the temptations and problems of this life.

Yes, some people are more gruff and prickly when they start with Jesus than others. Some people have been raised in more refined settings and may look like they have less to work on. But Jesus Christ works on and in all of us to get at the core selfishness that destroys the potential of our lives and disconnects us from God.

We will never be perfect until God takes us to Heaven and finishes our final preparation on that final day. But we can and will enjoy significant progress in our lives towards the image of Christ as long as we do not resist His work in us.

Consummation — Heaven:

At the end of our earthly life, God takes us to Heaven and finishes the job of bringing us to perfection and spiritual maturity. We will spend eternity with Him in Heaven.

I John 3:2

Beloved, now we are children of God, and it has not appeared as yet what we shall be. We know that, when He appears, we shall be like Him, because we shall see Him just as He is.

Notice that God will finish the process of making us fit for Heaven on the last day when we shall see Him face to face. He will make us like Himself so that we can enjoy the wonders of eternity and begin this second life, which will be our real life. You could think of the life we are living here as just a warm up for that one.

What Happens When You Become a Christian?

It is very helpful to look more closely at what happens when we ask Jesus Christ to become our Savior and Lord. Someone wrote down the number of promises and blessings that are bestowed upon us when we become Christians—there are over 5,000 of them documented in Scripture!

The following is a list of various promises, positions, and powers that become true for a person when they become a Christian. Some of these we feel; some are waiting for us to activate their power; others are waiting for us to discover their truth. Each of these can help us live different types of lives that glorify God. I have listed the verses where these truths are mentioned in Scripture.

These are not all of the things that happen to a person when they become a Christian, but they are highlights.

1. You become a child of God. (JOHN 1:12)

2. Christ becomes your friend. (JOHN 15:15)

3. You are declared righteous, forgiven for your sins against a holy God. (ROMANS 5:1)

4. You are united with Jesus Christ and move into a union with Him. (1 CORINTHIANS 6:7)

5. You have been bought for an immeasurable sum—the death of Christ. (1 CORINTHIANS 6:20)

6. You belong to God. (1 CORINTHIANS 6:19,20)

7. You are a member of Christ's body, the Church. (1 CORINTHIANS 12:27)

8. You have been given special abilities to serve Christ effectively. (1 CORINTHIANS 12:7)

9. You are a saint. (EPHESIANS 1:1)

10. You have been adopted as God's child. (EPHESIANS 1:5)

11. You have direct access to God through Jesus Christ by the Holy Spirit. (EPHESIANS 2:18)

12. You have been redeemed and forgiven of all your sins. (COLOSSIANS 1:14)

13. Christ has made you complete in Him; He is watching over you. (COLOSSIANS 2:10)

14. You are free forever from condemnation. (ROMANS 8:1,2)

15. You are assured that no matter what God allows to happen to you, He will work it out for your good and His glory. (ROMANS 8:28)

16. You have been bought out of the slave market of sin; you do not have to give into the temptations of the past. (ROMANS 6:10-14)

17. God will no longer listen to condemning charges against you. (ROMANS 8:31)

18. Nothing can separate you from God's love. (ROMANS 8:35)

19. You are established, anointed, and sealed by God. (2 CORINTHIANS 1:21,22)

20. God will not stop working on you to make you like Christ. (PHILIPPIANS 1:6)

21. You are a citizen of Heaven; home is in a new place. (PHILIPPIANS 3:20)

22. You can overcome fear through the power of God's love in you. (1 TIMOTHY 2:7)

23. You can always find more favor from God to help in your times of need. (HEBREWS 4:16)

24. You are born of God and the evil one cannot touch you with a destructive touch. (1 JOHN 5:18)

25. You have become salt and light to those who are without Christ. (MATTHEW 5:13,14)

26. You are a branch of the true vine, carrying the love, wisdom, and truth of God. (JOHN 15:1,5)

27. You have been chosen and appointed to bear fruit for God. (JOHN 15:16)

28. You are a personal witness of what Christ has done and is doing. (ACTS 1:8)

29. You have become a temple of the Almighty God living within you. (1 CORINTHIANS 6:19)

30. You are a consultant to others regarding how to be reconnected to God. (2 CORINTHIANS 5:17)

31. You are God's co-worker, cooperating with Him in His work. (1 CORINTHIANS 3:9; 2 CORINTHIANS 6:1)

32. You have a position of honor and privilege in Heaven because of Christ's love. (EPHESIANS 2:6)

33. You have been and will be given special good works to

do to demonstrate Christ is in your life, and you will give Him glory. (EPHESIANS 2:10)

34. You can always approach God through Christ even if you stumble. (EPHESIANS 3:12)

35. Christ gives you the strength and ability to do anything He wants. (PHILIPPIANS 4:13)

(This list has been adapted from Neil Andersen's lectures and books Bondage Breakers and Victory over Darkness.)

What Are Evidences of True Conversion and Salvation?

When a person becomes a Christian, something supernatural happens. Salvation actually changes a person. It begins a process that brings about a whole new person on the inside (2 CORINTHIANS 5:17). In Christ, the new person responds to God and to his or her surroundings entirely differently than the way they responded before. This is just like a lottery winner responding differently to everything in their lives. The new Christian has won the spiritual lottery. They have been forgiven of their sins and given a new relationship with God Almighty. They have the Holy Spirit to guide them, and promises of protection, provision, and opportunities that were not there before conversion. They have a new home in Heaven, where they will live someday.

True conversion can be evidenced by some new responses and changes in thinking. Below are some of the changes that accompany real conversion.

A New Love for Scripture

A new Christian will have a new excitement about hearing, reading, and/or studying Scripture, even if they may not enjoy reading. They develop a new love for God's love letters. I would describe this as a "hunger and thirst for the Word of God," like an insatiable desire to know more. This phenomenon is one of the clearest evidences of a true conversion of the Holy Spirit at work within them.

1 Peter 2:2

Like newborn babies, long for the pure milk of the word,
that by it you may grow in respect to salvation.

Notice that the Bible tells us that new Christians will want to take in the pure milk of the Word of God, just as new babies desperately want to have milk from their mothers. Expect that God will put within you an urge to read, hear, study, and/or talk about the Bible.

I have had the privilege of watching many people become Christians and have seen this urge in them to take in the Bible. I remember one woman told me that before she became a Christian, she did not ever read and doubted this would happen to her. But after she asked Jesus Christ to be her Savior and Lord, she developed an insatiable appetite for the Bible. She read through the verses and books of the Bible I suggested to her, and she kept asking for more. She admitted that this was new for her, but she felt it and wanted to know more about the Savior and this life He was leading her into.

Yes, it is possible to resist this urge to read and study the Bible, but it will leave your new life in Christ malnourished and too weak to really affect your life in the full way that God wants. Listen and heed the urge to read the Scriptures. Take the time to set aside a daily time with God, where you will prayerfully read and study the Word of God.

A few good places to start reading the Bible are:
- The Book of Philippians
- The Gospel of John
- The Book of James
- The Sermon on the Mount: MATTHEW 5-7
- The Book of Romans 1
- The Book of 1 Corinthians
- The Book of 1 John

Each of these books will be listed in the table of contents in your Bible as a part of the New Testament. The page numbers will be listed there. These books are not sequential and can be read in any order. They all fit together so go ahead and jump into reading the New Testament. Do not feel like you have to read them in order. Just jump right in, picking up any one of these New Testament books and start to prayerfully read. There are a lot of digital and online versions of the Bible, as well. I recommend You Version, which is free and available for your mobile device.

The following are a few Scriptures that Christians have found very helpful to memorize. Memorization is not difficult and there is a method to do it effectively. Just read the verse over and over again out loud until you can say it without looking. This usually takes between 10-20 times of reading a verse out loud.

Some people just write the verse they want to memorize on a card that they will carry with them during the day. It is perfectly okay if you forget the verse after a few days as you move on to other verses. God can bring the verse back to your memory when it is important for you. These verses would be great ones to focus on one day at a time:

- Romans 10:9
- 1 John 1:9
- Galatians 2:20
- Luke 9:23
- Philippians 1:6

A New Awareness of Right and Wrong

Those who come to Christ, sincerely giving their lives to Him, are given the gift of the Holy Spirit. The Holy Spirit brings a new awareness of what is right and what is wrong. Often people remark that things that seemed weird before they became a Christian, now feel like the right thing to do—helping others, going to church, talking about God, reading the Bible, etc. It is also true that the Holy Spirit brings a new kind of warning system that makes a person much more sensitive to what is wrong. Some have said, "I don't know why, but I can't do that anymore; it just seems wrong now."

Hebrews 5:13,14

For everyone who partakes only of milk is not accustomed to the word of righteousness, for he is a babe. But solid food is for the mature, who because of practice, have their senses trained to discern good and evil.

Notice that when you become a Christian, God begins to work in you to be aware of what is right and what is wrong. We become sensitized to things that harm others and are destructive even though they are acceptable in our culture.

I have talked with many people who, after their conversion to Christianity, tell me that they suddenly became aware of how selfish or harmful some activity truly was. Some will even say that they never gave some activities a second thought before, but now they realize that it is oppressive or destructive. The God of all righteousness has been invited into your life, and you are beginning to be in tune with His heart for people.

A New Desire to Be Like Jesus Christ

A person who invites Jesus Christ into his or her life to be Savior and Lord gains a new desire and power to be like Christ. God wants to live through you and allow you to enjoy life with a whole new perspective. This includes behavioral changes and a desire to learn more about Jesus Christ. There are three places in Scripture about the qualities of Christ and the Holy Spirit. Read and memorize them:

- Matthew 5:3-12
- Galatians 5:22,23
- 2 Peter 1:5-7

ROMANS 8:29

For whom He foreknew, He also predestined to become conformed to the image of His Son, that He might be the first-born among many brethren.

GALATIANS 5:22,23

But the fruit of the Spirit is love, joy, peace, patience, kindness, goodness, faithfulness, gentleness, self-control; against such things there is no law.

Notice that God wants you to express the character of Jesus Christ through the uniqueness of your life, personality, and experiences. God the Holy Spirit will begin to prompt you to be loving, joyful, or gentle when you would have been the opposite before. Listen to these new promptings to be a God-honoring version of yourself. When people begin to see the character and love of Jesus Christ coming through your words, actions, and attitudes, you'll know that your life is moving up to the next level.

A New Social Pressure from those Convicted by Your Changed Life

A new Christian can expect to receive some ridicule or even persecution from others for becoming "religious" or for living differently than everyone else. This rejection is to be expected, but also welcomed. It is not a sign that something is wrong, but rather that something is right. When people notice a change in you and put you to the test, it is evidence that your conversion is real. In fact, some non-Christians want to put a new Christian's faith immediately to the test by tempting them to do things that "Christians" shouldn't do. Follow your instincts and resist.

I PETER 4:3-5

For the time already past is sufficient for you to have carried out the desire of the Gentiles, having pursued a course of sensuality, lusts, drunkenness, carousals, drinking parties and abominable idolatries. And in all this, they are surprised that you do not run with them into the same excess of dissipation, and they malign you; but they shall give account to Him who is ready to judge the living and the dead.

Notice that people who become Christians feel the pull toward their new life, away from their old life, whatever that entailed. This pull to the new life often causes people from the old life to be upset or oppositional. This is normal and should be expected. Your old friends can sense the difference. You don't want to do the same things as before. You don't talk the same as before. You don't have the same attitude or reactions as before. You may not see it, but they do. This is Jesus in your life changing you.

I can remember talking to one man who said that he lost many of his friends because he no longer wanted to go drinking, partying, and visiting the strip clubs. He just didn't feel like it since he had become a Christian. He even tried to do these things with his buddies just like before, but it wasn't the same. He was more interested in other more righteous things and his old friends weren't ready for that kind of change.

Another man I talked to said that the people at work began to immediately pick on him because he was acting differently, even though he had specifically not told them that he had become a Christian. They said that he wasn't as cynical; he didn't tell dirty jokes like before; he was different and they no longer knew what to expect from him. When he finally did tell them that he became a Christian, they were even more open about their dislike of these changes. They told him that it wouldn't last and to stay away until this phase was over. They tried to tempt him to do things that would break this new source of purity and graciousness in his life.

A New Desire to Proclaim Christ to Others

Those who have really found Jesus Christ have a well of joy springing up within them, and they can hardly keep quiet about it. They want to tell everyone about the reality of the spiritual world, the wonder of Christ, the joy of knowing their sins are forgiven, the power of prayer, and the gentle guidance of the Holy Spirit.

ACTS 1:8

But you shall receive power when the Holy Spirit has come upon you; and you shall be My witnesses both in Jerusalem, and in all Judea and Samaria, and even to the remotest part of the earth.

COLOSSIANS 1:28

And we proclaim Him, admonishing every man and teaching every man with all wisdom, that we may present every man complete in Christ.

Notice that when a person becomes a Christian, there is a natural desire to tell other people about what has happened to you. If Jesus Christ has actually been invited into your life and has started to make changes on the inside, it is almost impossible to keep quiet about what is happening.

Yes, some people who are new Christians are not very tactful in telling other people about what Jesus is doing in their life, but it is okay. They may not be sensitive to the fact that the other person is not ready to respond to God, or that God is not calling out to that person at that moment in their life for a variety of reasons. But they have found the source of life and want others to experience it as well.

When we find a good movie or a good auto mechanic or a great restaurant, we have a hard time not telling people about it. Even more so when we invite God to come into our lives and He begins to make powerful, undeniable changes to our lives. We usually cannot shut up about what He is doing in us.

A New Love for Other Christians

Christians automatically have a concern and love for other Christians. This often comes as a shock to new Christians, as they have not necessarily enjoyed Christians before this time. But truly converted people want to hang around with other truly converted people who love Jesus. A small group of equally committed people is ideal for new Christians to express and receive love from Christians.

1 JOHN 3:14

We know that we have passed out of death into life, because we love the brethren. He who does not love abides in death.

Notice that when a person becomes a Christian, they have a new love for other true believers. Something inside of us reaches out and finds a kinship with other people who also love Jesus Christ. One of the key hallmarks of the life of Jesus Christ in us is this desire to love others (meet their needs, pursue them, and even please them).

I remember one man who said, "I always avoided Christians in the past because they were just too weird for me. But now I find I like hanging out with Christians." What was weird before may become much more acceptable once you have Jesus Christ in your life helping you see people differently.

What Causes Doubts about Our Salvation?

Misunderstanding Salvation

We must see salvation as the process of pardon for a sinner. Some people think they are saved because they started to go to church, or because they believe that Jesus is the Savior of the World, or because they lead a good life. Some people think that salvation is adding Jesus to their present life, or pledging to lead a good life from now on, or a willingness to pay for past sins. Salvation is none of these things. Salvation is surrender to Jesus Christ as your personal payment for sin and your personal boss for the rest of your life.

> I TIMOTHY 1:15
>
> *It is a trustworthy statement, deserving full acceptance that Christ Jesus came into the world to save sinners.*

Failing to Grow

If we fail to grow in our Christian life, then God predicts that we will become spiritually blind and lack the insight necessary to determine our own salvation. Second Peter 1:4-10 says that if we don't grow in Christ, then we will have persistent doubts about whether we are really Christian.

> 2 PETER 1:4-10
>
> *For by these He has granted to us His precious and magnificent promises, in order that by them you might become partakers of the divine nature, having escaped the corruption that is in the world by lust. Now for this very reason also, applying all diligence, in your faith supply moral excellence, and in you moral excellence,*

knowledge; and in your knowledge, self-control, and in your self-control, perseverance, and in your perseverance, godliness; and in your godliness brotherly kindness and in your brotherly kindness, love. For if these qualities are yours and are increasing, they render you neither useless nor unfruitful in the true knowledge of our Lord Jesus Christ. For he who lacks these qualities is blind or short-sighted, having forgotten his purification from his former sins. Therefore, brethren, be all the more diligent to make certain about His calling and choosing you; for as long as you practice these things you will never stumble;

Lacking a Birthdate

Many people doubt their salvation because they don't have a specific date when they surrendered their life to Jesus Christ as their personal Savior and Lord. It can be very helpful to clear up any birthdate problems by establishing today's date as your birthdate through personal surrender to Jesus Christ. Pray a prayer of surrender to Jesus Christ as your Savior and Lord today.

Mark down today's date in your Bible, in this book, or on the calendar so that there is no mystery about when you gave your life to Jesus Christ.

You can pray this prayer:
Dear Lord Jesus,

I want to become a Christian. I realize that I can't earn my way into heaven or a relationship with you. I need you to save me from my sins and my inability to maintain a relationship with you. I thank you for dying on the cross for me. If I never did it right before, I do surrender my life to the Lord Jesus Christ as my only hope of heaven. Come into my life and make me the kind of person you want me to be.

In the Name of the Lord Jesus Christ,

Amen

Harboring Bitterness

Many people cannot sense Christ's forgiveness because they are unwilling to let go of a bitterness or offense they are holding on to. MATTHEW 6:12, 14-15 tells us that we will sense or experience the forgiveness of God based upon our willingness to forgive those who have offended us. Some people sense that if they were to truly come to Christ for forgiveness, they would eventually need to learn how to forgive the people who deeply hurt them. It is true that Christians learn how to let go of bitterness and allow any justice to be handled by God and the proper authorities. It is liberating to not let what someone else did to you be a major player in your life. Yes, people can do terrible things to each other. But God can turn their wrong into blessings.

MATTHEW 6:12-15

And forgive us our debts, as we also have forgiven our debtors. And do not lead us into temptation, but deliver us from evil. [For Thine is the kingdom, and the power, and the glory, forever. Amen]. For if you forgive men for their transgressions, your heavenly Father will also forgive you. But if you do not forgive men, then your Father will not forgive your transgressions.

A Deep Sense of Worthlessness

Some people can't feel that God has loved them if they have never been unconditionally or deeply loved by someone else first. They may consistently doubt their salvation until someone loves them unconditionally, or they make a deep personal spiritual connection with the Lord Jesus Christ over a long period of time. Then by faith in what God says in the Bible, they understand and believe that they are saved by the work of Jesus Christ. They have to feel love to believe that they are worthy of being loved. It must be demonstrated to them or they can't really envision themselves being loved. Allow Christ to love you. Taste and see that the Lord is good.

Become a Christian by Making a Trade with God!

God has offered to make one of the most lopsided trades of all time. In order to appreciate the trade that He offers, a person must understand Heaven's requirements. In order to earn your way into Heaven, you need to be absolutely perfect (MATTHEW 5:48; EZEKIEL 18:4). No one has ever lived a perfect life on earth except Jesus Christ. Everyone falls short of the perfection needed to earn his or her way into Heaven (ROMANS 3:23). Heaven must therefore be a gift. God, in His wisdom, grace, and mercy, developed and carried out a plan to give Heaven as a free gift to all those who would fully embrace Him as their God. He sent His Son to the earth to be born of a virgin. His Son lived a perfect life with no sin. He, therefore, qualified for Heaven. God's Son, Jesus Christ, willingly gave up His perfect life to trade it for those who could not qualify for Heaven on their own. (2 CORINTHIANS 5:17)

When a person embraces Jesus Christ as their Savior and Lord, they are basically making a trade between themselves and God. They are trading all their sin and rebellion for Jesus' perfection and favor with God. A person who wants to be a Christian and be in favor with God needs to admit that they are not perfect and can never earn their way into God's favor or Heaven. A person who wants to be a Christian also must admit that they need a Savior, who will pay for their sins and extend grace (a privileged position) to them. A person who wants to be a Christian needs to declare to God and others (ROMANS 10:9) that they are trusting Jesus Christ and His death on the cross as their only way to Heaven.

A person who wants to be a Christian needs to surrender their life to Jesus Christ so that He can make them the kind of person that He wants them to be. A person who wishes to be a Christian must understand that they are making a trade with God: You trade your sin, mistakes, wrong doings, and imperfections for Jesus Christ's perfection, love, and favor with God. Jesus also becomes the boss of your life as you become a follower of His… growing in His favor and understanding how He wants you to live your life.

Let's suppose that you were married and your spouse is absolutely perfect. He or she dies and goes to Heaven. When she gets there, the pearly gates swing wide open. She enjoys the benefits and blessing of Heaven because she has lived an absolutely perfect life.

Now, let's suppose that while your spouse is in Heaven, he remembers you on Earth. He knows that you can't earn your way into Heaven because you are not perfect like he is. So he goes to God and proposes a trade. He will trade all of his perfection to you and you will give him all your sins. God agrees, as long as you agree.

So she comes back and informs you about this trade. She tells you about how wonderful Heaven is and how much she wants you to enjoy it. You agree to trade all your sin and wrong for her perfection. Now when you approach the gates of Heaven, they swing wide open for you, because you are now perfect.

The only problem is that there is still only one person in Heaven, you. God loves the whole world and wants Heaven to be available to everyone (2 PETER 3:9). So it can't just be a man or a woman who lives a perfect life and gives it up for another. It must be God, who became a man, lived a perfect life, and then gave up His life. Then the trade could be offered to everyone, because his life can never end. As many as are willing to trade their sins for Christ's perfection can be given entrance into Heaven.

Part of the trade is that Jesus Christ becomes our Lord and Master; in other words, there is a complete surrender to the One who was willing to take our sins. He made Him who knew no sin to be sin on our behalf that we might become the righteousness of God. (2 CORINTHIANS 5:21) But to as many as received Him, He gave them the right to be the children of God. (JOHN 1:12)

Have You Made the Trade?

The trade is made through prayer, talking to God. A prayer to make the trade goes something like this:

Dear Heavenly Father,

I realize that I am a sinner and not perfect enough to earn my way into Heaven. I need your payment for my sins. I thank you that through the Lord Jesus Christ's death on the cross I can be fully forgiven. I want to right now make this trade with Christ. I want Christ to take all my sins and I want to receive His perfection.

I realize that when I make this trade it means that I want Jesus Christ to run my life. I also give you permission to make me the kind of person you want me to be. I thank you Lord Jesus for dying on the cross for my sins. I want you, Jesus, to make me the kind of person you want me to be.

In Jesus Christ's Name,

Amen

FOUNDATIONS

BUILDING BLOCK #2

Growing as a Follower of Christ

Building Block #2
Growing as a Follower of Christ

Becoming a Christian essentially means that you are committing to following Christ, which involves learning how to live and think like Christ. A Christ follower begins a spiritual journey that allows Jesus to transform his or her life, starting from the inside out. Internal changes occur inside a person (heart, soul, mind) and then practiced out in the real world as we interact with others. Many people have the mistaken idea that the outward changes occur first, or they themselves can change by their own power. But the change begins internally once a person accepts Christ as their Lord and Savior. The transformation of what a person can become as they let Christ lead is a process of learning, practicing, and developing. The result will be pleasing to God, to those around you, and to yourself. Welcome to the spiritual journey!

Christ followers move forward in this journey by learning how Jesus wants them to live and think so that they can fulfill their destiny and deepen their relationship with God. This is the next natural step after asking Jesus Christ to be your Savior and your Lord. Jesus tells us a number of times in Scripture that He wants His followers to be disciples and also to go and make disciples. The word DISCIPLE means to be a learner. Christ wants people to learn from Him and to pass what we learn on to others. As we get started in our Christian life, there are many things to learn about how to live and think like a Christian. But the wonderful thing is that

God has given us all we need in the Bible and the church to learn Christ's ways. Look at what Jesus says about learning from Him.

MATTHEW 11:28-30

Come to Me, all who are weary and heavy-laden, and I will give you rest. Take My yoke upon you and learn from Me, for I am gentle and humble in heart, and you will find rest for your souls. For My yoke is easy and My burden is light.

Notice that in these verses Jesus says when you come to Him, He will give you rest. He will teach you a new way of living and responding to life. His ways are easy and they aren't burdensome. He wants to introduce us to a way of living and thinking that is different from the competitive pressures of the world. In another passage, Jesus tells us more about becoming a follower of Christ (a disciple or a learner).

MATTHEW 28:18-20

And Jesus came up and spoke to them, saying, "All authority has been given to Me in heaven and on earth. Go, therefore, and make disciples of all the nations, baptizing them in the name of the Father and the Son and the Holy Spirit, teaching them to observe all that I commanded you; and lo, I am with you always, even to the end of the age."

Notice that in this passage that being a Christ follower or disciple involves two things:
- Being baptized;
- Becoming a person who begins to live and think Jesus' way.

What Is Baptism?

The word baptism means to *dip* or *immerse*. To illustrate this concept, imagine a candle maker dipping a wick into wax, or the process of dying clothes by dipping them into a colored solution. Christian baptism means to be immersed in water to symbolize acceptance of Jesus Christ as Savior and Lord.

Why Do Christians Baptize?

Jesus Christ commanded that believers be baptized. (MATTHEW 28:18-20) In taking part in baptism, one joins the company of believers throughout history, who have placed their hope of Heaven in the life and death of Jesus Christ. God gives this identification mark as a way to say that a person has moved past the curious stage in regards to Christ. While there are various Christian controversies over how to baptize and when to baptize, the point is that Christians baptize. Jesus Christ, the apostles, and the early church saw baptism as an essential discipline or step for compliance to God's commands.

What Are the Three Truths Taught through Baptism?

To be baptized symbolizes three distinct truths about being a Christian.

The Tri-Unity of God
One distinctive of the Christian faith is that it perceives three distinct persons within the One being of God. Baptism means to embrace

the tri-unity of God and become a follower of the teachings of Jesus. (MATTHEW 4:18-19; 28:18-20; 20:28) This unity and diversity within God is absolutely different from any other religious faith. Jesus indicated that baptism was to picture this truth by stating that disciples were to be baptized into the one name of the Father, Son, and Holy Spirit. To be baptized means there is an acceptance of God as not just a singularity, but as *three in one*. A second idea contained in this triune embrace is that the Christian accepts that Jesus' teachings about life are the correct perspective on life. A Christian accepts God as three in one and is dedicated to learning the way Jesus wants a person to live life.

Death and Resurrection

Baptism means accepting a voluntary death to selfishness and a rebirth to life under new conditions. (ROMANS 6:1-4) The apostle Paul, writing under the inspiration of the Holy Spirit, states that those who have been baptized into Christ have been baptized into His death. The Christian is willing to die to his selfish and self-centered way of life and follow God's new way of life. Baptism is the outward ceremony of an inward decision to live this new way of life and a willingness to live this way for the rest of our lives.

The sixth chapter of Romans states that we should no longer go on presenting the parts of our body as tools for selfishness, but instead we should present our bodies to God as instruments of righteousness. Being baptized means that we recognize our life is not our own but instead a part of Christ's work in the world. If people cannot accept this way of life, then they do not fully understand what it means to be a Christian and are not ready to be baptized.

Cleansing

Baptism is also a picture of a dirty person inside a bathtub with soap and a scrub brush. In 1 PETER 3:21, God says that baptism is an appeal to God for a clean conscience. This perspective demonstrates a Christian's willingness to be made clean by God from the stain of sin. Baptism is a way of saying to God in ceremonial form that we want Him to take a scrub brush to our souls. Most people innately realize that in order to be in the presence of a holy God, they must be clean and pure. The problem is how.

Jesus Christ has given us a way to be clean before God. Jesus paid for our sins and acts as our substitute for our penalties. Baptism is a way of declaring that we desire in our inner most parts to be clean and pure. If people are not willing to admit that they are selfish, sinful, and morally dirty in their soul, having offended the holy God of the Bible, then they are not ready to be baptized.

To sum up, baptism is a picture of three different things. It is a sacred ceremony marking three crucial steps of the beginning of the Christian Life.

1. It is a belief in God as *three in one*—Father, Son, Holy Spirit. (MATTHEW 28:18-20)
2. It is a death to your old way of selfish living and a pledge of obedience to God's positive and negative commands of love. (ROMANS 6:1-5)
3. It is a sincere request for God to cleanse your soul of your sins by applying your guilt to Jesus Christ and His death on the cross. (1 PETER 3:21)

What Does Baptism Accomplish?

Some have erroneously contended that baptism actually regenerates or saves a person. This is not true. *Belief* alone is the catalyst for salvation and regeneration. But baptism does accomplish a number of very significant things in the life of the believer.

1. Baptism seals or marks a person's salvation God's way. (MATTHEW 28:18-20)
2. Baptism gives a measure of God's invisible grace, just as every act of obedience to any of God's revealed commands increases the grace of God in our lives.
3. Baptism is a powerful testimony of our seriousness to die to our old life and our desire to live a new life under the direction of Jesus Christ. (ROMANS 6:1-4)
4. Baptism proclaims the sacrifice Christ made for our sins, and the fact that we are no longer under the condemnation of God's wrath for our sins and rebellion. (ROMANS 8:1,2-11)
5. Baptism provides an opportunity to proclaim to our loved ones and the whole human race that we understand and accept the responsibility of being a Christian and loving Jesus Christ. *(Spiritual Disciplines of a C.H.R.I.S.T.I.A.N., by Gil Stieglitz, pp. 190-192.)*

If you haven't yet been baptized but are ready to take that step, schedule it with your church or a pastor or friend. Then you can begin inviting your friends, relatives, and colleagues to come and watch you take this significant spiritual step.

What Is Involved in Learning to Live and Think as a Christian?

Jesus Christ has a way to live a life that is full of love and significance, and He wants us to follow Him into it. Christians have been helping other Christians use the Bible to follow Jesus since He rose again and ascended to Heaven. Since Jesus left almost 2,000 years ago, Christian scholars have been describing what being a disciple means as two things: 1) learning to live how Jesus would want us to live, and 2) learning how to think how Jesus would want us to think. The theological terms for these ideas are Orthopraxy (Christian living) and Orthodoxy (Christian thinking).

Let's describe these two ideas (Orthopraxy and Orthodoxy) in further detail. Christian living (Orthopraxy) involves learning

Discipleship

Orthodoxy 10 Truths	Orthopraxy 10 Relationships
God	Spirituality
Jesus	Self
Holy Spirit	Marriage
Bible	Family
Salvation (Success)	Work
Mankind (Spirituality)	Church
Angels	Money
Church	Friends
After Life	Community
End Times	Enemies

Jesus' principles for all ten major relationships of life. Christian thinking (Orthodoxy) means learning Jesus' truths about the ten spiritual realities that make up a Christian worldview. We will be learning about these two aspects of the Christian life for the rest of our lives here on earth. The deeper we go and the more obedient we become, the deeper our transformation will be into God-honoring Christians.

God has a wonderful plan for us. (EPHESIANS 2:10; JOHN 10:10) All we need to do is to begin learning how to live out God's plan. He has good works, adventures, relationships, and accomplishments in mind for each of us. The more we know about Jesus' way of living and thinking, the more we will be able fulfill the destiny that God has in mind for us. Notice what God tells us about the plan He has for our life in these two Scriptures:

EPHESIANS 2:10

For we are His workmanship, created in Christ Jesus for good works, which God prepared beforehand, that we should walk in them.

JOHN 10:10

I came that they might have life, and might have it abundantly.

What Is Christian Orthopraxy?

Usually Christian Orthopraxy is described as learning Jesus' way of living in the ten major relationships of life. The Bible is full of powerful instructions on how to make those relationships work and be filled with love. These include your relationship with God, self, marriage, family, work, money (finances, possessions), friends, church, community, and enemies. Let's go through each relationship and define each of them.

Discipleship

Orthopraxy
10 Major Relationships
God
Self
Marriage
Family
Work
Money
Friends
Church
Community
Enemies

Your Relationship with God, or Spirituality

God wants to be in relationship with you. He wants to go deeper in revealing Himself to you, guiding you, and interacting with you. Your relationship with God is a highly personal process. There are spiritual exercises and pathways talked about in the Bible that have been helping people love God and be loved by Him for 2,000 years. Since our relationship with God is foundational, let's go a little deeper in our discussion of this relationship. We have found it very helpful to let Christians know that they must spend time maintaining and developing their relationship with God. If you have accepted Jesus Christ as your Savior and Lord, your relationship with God has started, and it is now time to move forward in that relationship. Jesus has provided all the grace and forgiveness needed, but you do need to pursue the relationship. Here is how.

What should you do during your time with God every day?

Most Christians have found that having a close and developing relationship with Jesus Christ requires a half an hour to an hour set aside each day to focus on God, as well as lots of little prayers throughout the day. I usually suggest that a Christian work through various spiritual exercises during this time so that they can hear from the Lord and keep their spiritual life tuned up and growing. I recommend using the acrostic C.H.R.I.S.T. Each one of these stands for a type of spiritual exercise that will help you practice your faith and hopefully put you in God's presence.

Confession

This entails taking the time to ask God if you have been displeasing to Him in some way. Serious Christians down through the centuries have spent time every day letting God bring up stuff that He wants us to change. God is never condemning in these times, because He has already paid for the problem through the death of His Son, Jesus Christ. But He wants to guide us away from the issues of selfishness, rebellion, and sin that are keeping us from the life He really wants us to live. Ask God to bring to your mind actions, words, or emotions that have been particularly displeasing to Him. Agree with God and thank Him for forgiving you for your sins already in Jesus' death on the cross. Ask Him for the power to turn away from those sins in the future. (1 JOHN 1:9)

Like King David, who cried out to the Lord in PSALM 139:23,24, you can too:

"Search me, O God, and know my heart; Try me and know my anxious thoughts; And see if there be any hurtful way in me, And lead me in the everlasting way."

The Apostle John had the same idea in 1 JOHN 1:9:

"If we confess our sins He is faithful and righteous to forgive us of all our sins and cleanse us from all unrighteousness."

Confession means that we can keep short accounts with God of the ways that we have resisted Him, have been selfish, or hurtful to others.

Holy Spirit

The Holy Spirit is one of the great blessings of being a Christian. God will prompt us, urge us, and suggest to us that we act in loving and kind ways to others. Once a person becomes a Christian they will "sense" these urges more clearly. The more that we listen and do what He is asking us to do, the more we will be filling our life with His love. He wants you to be an agent of His love and joy to the people in your life.

The Holy Spirit has come to guide us through life, apply the Bible, warn us of temptations, and prompt us into loving action. Each day, the Holy Spirit will work within our conscience to move us in the right direction. (GALATIANS 5:16; EPHESIANS 4:30; 5:18) We know that God the Holy Spirit will apply the truth of the Scripture to our heart to guide our conscience. So expect that God the Holy Spirit will prompt you to apply the Scripture(s) you are reading. Also, we know that God the Holy Spirit seeks to produce certain qualities in our life. These qualities are called the *Fruit of the Holy Spirit*. GALATIANS 5:22,23 tells us that He will prompt you to exercise the fruit of the spirit throughout various parts of the day—that is love, joy, peace, patience, kindness, goodness, gentleness, and self-control. He will prompt you to participate in these activities every day. As you are alert to the Holy Spirit's prompting, your life will take on a Christ-like character. It has been helpful for many to memorize the Fruit of the Spirit verses so you can be ready for God's direction.

GALATIANS 5:22-23

"But the fruit of the Spirit is love, joy, peace, patience, kindness, goodness, faithfulness, gentleness and self-control. Against such things there is no law."

THE FRUIT OF THE HOLY SPIRIT:
- **LOVE:** meeting needs; pursuing; pleasing
- **JOY:** deepen relationships and a positive orientation to life
- **PEACE:** stop making war with God or others; repair past conflicts
- **PATIENCE:** give God and others more time to work
- **KINDNESS:** treating people with pleasant helpfulness
- **GOODNESS:** doing that which is truly beneficial for

God and others
- **MEEKNESS:** gentleness, impulse control, and controlled energy
- **FAITHFULNESS:** perseverance toward a righteous goal
- **SELF-CONTROL:** moderation in all things; control of passions within proper limits

Reading and Repetition

Since we want a special relationship with Jesus Christ, then we need to take some time every day to spend time with Him. He has written us a special letter about who He is and what He wants us to do—that is, the Bible. It is special because it tells us things that no other book tells us. The Bible is without error and has the life of God breathed into it. Its pages are inspired with His life. (2 TIMOTHY 3:14-17) Prayerfully read through a section of the Bible listening for God to highlight something, maybe a verse or part of a verse. Then begin to say that verse or part of the verse over and over again. Do this as you fall asleep and as you go throughout your day. This is called meditating.

Reading through the Bible is essential for maintaining a strong faith. Repeating Scripture throughout the day is a process of internalizing and thinking about what they mean. This keeps scriptural ideas and scriptural wisdom active in your decisions and interactions with people. Read a chapter or a paragraph of Scripture every day. Then repeat it throughout the day or for many days if you'd like.

Interaction: Bible Study and Prayer

To interact with God means that you speak with Him and He speaks back to you. Studying the Bible is probably the best way to hear from the Lord about your situation. When we take the time to study the Bible in depth, God's Spirit begins to speak to our needs. When we study a passage of Scripture, we are looking for God's mind and God's answers. Then we can ask God much more accurately about the issues on our mind. (LUKE 18:1)

Prayer is a dialogue with God. We can ask God for wisdom, strength, truth, provision, etc., and we can hear back from Him in a variety of ways—prayer, His Word, other believers, or circumstances. If we are to maintain a strong relationship with God we must speak to Him and listen hard for what He is saying to us. If there is no conversation with God, then there can be no relationship with God.

Service

Let God know that you are ready to serve Him in three ways:

    1) daily helping or aiding someone He may direct you to,

    2) in the church in some way, and

    3) in the community unleashing compassion.

If you are not serving Him daily, in the church, and in the community, then ask God to show you where you can make a difference. A rule of thumb is to serve at least two hours a week in the church and two hours a month in the community. (MATTHEW 4:10; MATTHEW 16:24)

Thankfulness

Spend some time thanking God for the blessings that He has brought into your life. Thank God for who He is and what He has done for you. Spend some time thanking God for salvation and the blessings of the Bible, friends, truth, etc. (PSALM 103:1-5)

> *(If you are interested in going through more of these exercises, I write about them in more detail in my book,* ***Spiritual Disciplines of a C.H.R.I.S.T.I.A.N.)***

Your Relationship with Yourself, or Personal Development

God wants you to be the best possible version of yourself that you can be spiritually, mentally, emotionally, and physically. Jesus wants you to embrace the abilities, gifts, talents, desires, and dreams that He has put within you for a truly significant and meaningful life.

Your Relationship with Your Spouse if You are Married, Were Married, or Plan to be Married

God's plan for many people (not everyone) is that they would be married. His desire for their marriage is that it would be a wonderful harmony between two people for emotional, financial, mental, relational, spiritual, and physical support. In the Scriptures, God has given lots of principles, commands, wisdom, and boundaries so that your marriage will be full of love and health.

Your Relationship with Your Family, Including Your Family of Origin and Immediate Family

Jesus wants you to learn how to take all of the good things about your family of origin and process through the bad in order to build a new family (nuclear and/or church family) that will encourage, support, and bring you joy. In the Bible, God has many instructions about how to strengthen your family skills, whether that is parenting, being a child, or being a sibling. He wants your relationships to be full of grace, mercy, and power as He pours into your life, instead of being one who is toxic to others.

Your Relationship with Your Work

Throughout the Scriptures God has given significant instructions and principles to improve the vocational area. Those who learn and follow God's commands in this area will see their career and/or vocational arena transform to be a source of light, joy, and love in their life. It is important to realize that God has not left us on our own in the vocational area. He knows how to transform us, and this whole area of work.

Your Relationship with Your Finances, Possessions, and Money

While this is not usually considered a relationship in the traditional sense, the Bible consistently declares that we all have a relationship with this financial part of our life. God declares that there are principles, commands, and wisdom to keep moving this part of your life forward with health, and not toxicity. It is amazing what happens when we follow what God says to do in the area of finances.

Your Relationship with Friends of All Types and Places

All of us need friends and have friends of all different levels, from acquaintances, to casual friends, to close friends, to deep friends.

God gives us many principles, commands, and wisdom in this area of friends so that they will be a benefit to our life and not a hindrance to the life we could enjoy.

Your Relationships with Your Church, the Group of Christians You Identify With, Worship With, and Receive Support from for Your Christian Life

There is no such thing as a healthy "Lone Ranger Christian." God knows that we all need other believers around us to help us, correct us, train us, delight in us, and inspire us. God's principles, commands, and wisdom about how to build a dynamic group of Christians will make a huge difference when followed. Your church supplies three critical elements to your spiritual life that can't come from anywhere else.

- The group worship experience.
- Your growth experiences in a group context.
- A large part of your serving opportunities to advance the cause of Christ.

It is important to find a church home and start growing roots. Get plugged in, serve, meet the people, and grow your relationships. This is another hallmark of the Christian life.

Your Relationship with Society, Community, City, and Nation

Everyone lives within a community or larger society. God has a lot to say about the ways we can cause our larger society to be a place of health and justice for all. When followed, His principles, commands, and wisdom in this area allow for a civil society that works and functions well, even though there will always be people on this earth who do evil actions within it. Our small part can make a big difference.

Your Relationship with Your Enemies.

Every Christian faces at least four different types of enemies throughout our lives that are made up of:

- Those we pick up because of foolish things we do;
- Those who are set against us because of the nature of the world we live in.

Throughout the Bible, God tells us how to handle these various enemies, who will pop into our life and try and opposes us, manipulate us, deceive us, and tempt us.

(I talk in depth about the four enemies of the Christian in my book,
Basic Spiritual Warfare.*)*

We constantly need to be learning Christ's ways in these relationships as our age and life stage bring new challenges to Christ's ways of living. Ask your church if it has groups, classes, counseling, and mentoring that can walk you through these various relationships until there is health, joy, and harmony in your life in these areas.

Do not be stressed that you do not already know all of these principles, commands, and wisdom. Being a Christ follower is to be a learner. Every Christian is learning how to follow Jesus in new ways. We are all learning how to let Christ guide us and direct us. Every year we are given fifty-two new weeks to learn more about following Jesus with our relationships and with our thinking.

What Is Christian Orthodoxy?

In order to begin thinking like a Christ follower, this requires that we begin to grow in our understanding of ten spiritual realties. It is these ten truths that begin to transform our thinking and allow us to please God with our lives at new levels. These ten truths have been called the pillars of Christian doctrine in the past, but they really form the foundation of Christian thinking. Many Christians have not been taught the intellectual basis of Christianity and the crucial ideas that form Christian thinking. This next section is an introduction to orthodoxy and Christian thinking. Learning about and incorporating these ten realities allows us to grow in our Christian lives and explain the world as it really is. In each case I have explained the Christian answer and have put verses of Scripture from which that answer has been derived. For a more detailed explanation and deeper discussion on the **Ten Big Questions of Life**, see *Appendix 1* in the back of the book.

Discipleship

Orthodoxy
10 Spiritual Realities
God
Jesus
Holy Spirit
Bible
Salvation (Success)
Mankind (Spiritual)
Angels
Church
After Life
End Times

What Are the Ten Spiritual Truths?

1. GOD: There is a God, a supreme being, who is outside our spatial and time dimension. He created our universe and the laws it operates by. He is perfect, almighty, all knowing, and wise, as well as holy, transcendent, and righteous.

Exodus 34:6,7

Then the LORD passed by in front of him and proclaimed, "The LORD, the LORD God, compassionate and gracious, slow to anger, and abounding in lovingkindness and truth; who keeps lovingkindness for thousands, who forgives iniquity, transgression and sin; yet He will by no means leave the guilty unpunished, visiting the iniquity of fathers on the children and on the grandchildren to the third and fourth generations."

Psalm 139:7-12

Where can I go from Your Spirit? Or where can I flee from Your presence? If I ascend to heaven, You are there; If I make my bed in Sheol, behold, You are there. If I take the wings of the dawn, If I dwell in the remotest part of the sea, Even there Your hand will lead me, And Your right hand will lay hold of me. If I say, "Surely the darkness will overwhelm me, And the light around me will be night," Even the darkness is not dark to You, And the night is as bright as the day. Darkness and light are alike to You.

Acts 17:24,25

The God who made the world and all things in it, since

He is Lord of heaven and earth, does not dwell in temples made with hands; nor is He served by human hands, as though He needed anything, since He Himself gives to all people life and breath and all things;

EXODUS 3:13-15

Then Moses said to God, "Behold, I am going to the sons of Israel, and I will say to them, 'The God of your fathers has sent me to you.' Now they may say to me, 'What is His name?' What shall I say to them?" God said to Moses, "I AM WHO I AM"; and He said, "Thus you shall say to the sons of Israel, 'I AM has sent me to you.'" God, furthermore, said to Moses, "Thus you shall say to the sons of Israel, 'The LORD, the God of your fathers, the God of Abraham, the God of Isaac, and the God of Jacob, has sent me to you.' This is My name forever, and this is My memorial-name to all generations."

2. JESUS: God became a man in order to show us what God was like and to save us from our selfishness. Jesus Christ lived the perfect life, qualified to enter Heaven, gave up His perfect life to willingly die in our place, and rose from the dead to prove that He had accomplished our salvation.

ISAIAH 9:6

For a child will be born to us, a son will be given to us; And the government will rest on His shoulders; And His name will be called Wonderful Counselor, Mighty God, Eternal Father, Prince of Peace.

LUKE 1:31-33

And behold, you will conceive in your womb and bear a son, and you shall name Him Jesus. He will be great and will be called the Son of the Most High; and the Lord God will give Him the throne of His father David; and He will reign over the house of Jacob forever, and His kingdom will have no end.

REVELATION 1:17,18

When I saw Him, I fell at His feet like a dead man. And He placed His right hand on me, saying, "Do not be afraid; I am the first and the last, and the living One; and I was dead, and behold, I am alive forevermore, and I have the keys of death and Hades."

3. HOLY SPIRIT: God has sent His Holy Spirit to live in every believer, guide them to do His will, support them in their journey through this life, and empower them with grace, gifts, and power to live for Christ.

ACTS 5:3-5

But Peter said, "Ananias, why has Satan filled your heart to lie to the Holy Spirit and to keep back some of the price of the land? While it remained unsold, did it not remain your own? And after it was sold, was it not under your control? Why is it that you have conceived this deed in your heart? You have not lied to men but to God." And as he heard these words, Ananias fell down and breathed his last; and great fear came over all who heard of it.

ISAIAH 11:2

The Spirit of the LORD will rest on Him, The Spirit of wisdom and understanding, The Spirit of counsel and strength, The Spirit of knowledge and the fear of the LORD.

JOHN 16:7-14

But I tell you the truth, it is to your advantage that I go away; for if I do not go away, the Helper will not come to you; but if I go, I will send Him to you. And He, when He comes, will convict the world concerning sin and righteousness and judgment; concerning sin, because they do not believe in Me; and concerning righteousness, because I go to the Father and you no longer see Me; and concerning judgment, because the ruler of this world has been judged. I have many more things to say to you, but you cannot bear them now. But when He, the Spirit of truth, comes, He will guide you into all the truth; for He will not speak on His own initiative, but whatever He hears, He will speak; and He will disclose to you what is to come. "He will glorify Me, for He will take of Mine and will disclose it to you.

4. THE BIBLE: God has given us a written communication about Him so that there would be no question about who He is and what He wants us from us. God's record of what He wanted us to know is called the Bible. He moved on and in over 40 human authors over the course of 2,000 years to write down particular stories, facts, and truths so that we would know about how to love Him, others, and ourselves righteously.

2 Timothy 3:16

All Scripture is inspired by God and profitable for teaching, for reproof, for correction, for training in righteousness.

Psalm 19:7-11

The law of the LORD is perfect, restoring the soul; The testimony of the LORD is sure, making wise the simple. The precepts of the LORD are right, rejoicing the heart; The commandment of the LORD is pure, enlightening the eyes. The fear of the LORD is clean, enduring forever; The judgments of the LORD are true; they are righteous altogether. They are more desirable than gold, yes, than much fine gold; sweeter also than honey and the drippings of the honeycomb. Moreover, by them Your servant is warned; In keeping them there is great reward.

1 Peter 1:20,21

For He was foreknown before the foundation of the world, but has appeared in these last times for the sake of you who through Him are believers in God, who raised Him from the dead and gave Him glory, so that your faith and hope are in God.

5. SALVATION: God has provided all we need to reconnect with Him and lead a truly successful life. Christian salvation is the pathway to a truly successful life. Jesus tells us that the greatest commandments are to love God, others, and ourselves righteously. Success in life is relational, not material.

Do you have a relationship with God?

Salvation is the act of God, whereby He invites the unworthy and incapable sinner to begin a loving relationship with Him through faith based upon the work that He did in the life, death, and resurrection of His Son, Jesus Christ. It results in learning how to love others at new levels and oneself in righteous ways.

The following is a prayer that can begin your life of faith in God.

> *Dear Heavenly Father,*
>
> *I come to you through the work of your only begotten Son, Jesus Christ. I admit that I am a sinner and have violated your rules and standards in my life. I need your gift of forgiveness in Jesus.*
>
> *I accept His payment for my sins. I ask Him to make me everything You want me to be.*
>
> *Thank You, Jesus, for dying on the cross for my sins. I believe in You as my only hope of Heaven and eternal life.*
>
> *Amen*

JOHN 1:29

The next day he saw Jesus coming to him and said, "Behold, the Lamb of God who takes away the sin of the world!"

ROMANS 3:21-27

But now apart from the Law the righteousness of God has been manifested, being witnessed by the Law and the Prophets, even the righteousness of God through faith in Jesus Christ for all those who believe; for there is no distinction; for all have sinned and fall short of the glory of God, being justified as a gift by His grace through the redemption which is in Christ Jesus; whom God displayed publicly as a propitiation in His blood through faith.

ROMANS 8:28-30

And we know that God causes all things to work together for good to those who love God, to those who are called according to His purpose. For those whom He foreknew, He also predestined to become conformed to the image of His Son, so that He would be the firstborn among many brethren; and these whom He predestined, He also called; and these whom He called, He also justified; and these whom He justified, He also glorified.

JEREMIAH 31:31-34

"Behold, days are coming," declares the LORD, "when I will make a new covenant with the house of Israel and with the house of Judah, not like the covenant which I made with their fathers in the day I took them by the hand to bring them out of the land of Egypt, My covenant which they broke, although I was a husband to them," declares the LORD. "But this is the covenant which I will make with the house of Israel after those days," declares the LORD, "I will put My law within them and on their heart I will write it; and I will be their God, and they shall be My people. "They will not teach again, each man his neighbor and each man his

brother, saying, 'Know the LORD,' for they will all know Me, from the least of them to the greatest of them," *declares the LORD, "for I will forgive their iniquity, and their sin I will remember no more."*

6. MANKIND: God tells us that we bear His image in the world and have been given the responsibility to steward this world well. He also tells us that our first parents chose to rebel from God's rulership of their lives and every one of us since that time has also chosen to rebel from God's direction and plan. This is why we have a broken and dysfunctional world that doesn't work. Our natural default setting is now selfishness, rather than goodness and peace.

Genesis 1:26,27

Then God said, "Let Us make man in Our image, according to Our likeness; and let them rule over the fish of the sea and over the birds of the sky and over the cattle and over all the earth, and over every creeping thing that creeps on the earth." God created man in His own image, in the image of God He created him; male and female He created them.

Romans 3:10-18

As it is written, "There is none righteous, not even one; there is none who understands, there is none who seeks for God; all have turned aside, together they have become useless; there is none who does good, there is not even one." "Their throat is an open grave, with their tongues they

KEEP DECEIVING," "THE POISON OF ASPS IS UNDER THEIR LIPS"; "WHOSE MOUTH IS FULL OF CURSING AND BITTERNESS"; "THEIR FEET ARE SWIFT TO SHED BLOOD, DESTRUCTION AND MISERY ARE IN THEIR PATHS, AND THE PATH OF PEACE THEY HAVE NOT KNOWN." "THERE IS NO FEAR OF GOD BEFORE THEIR EYES."

1 THESSALONIANS 5:23

Now may the God of peace Himself sanctify you entirely; and may your spirit and soul and body be preserved complete, without blame at the coming of our Lord Jesus Christ.

7. ANGELS: God tells us that there are other intelligent beings that He created. These were designed to serve His creation and us. Just like us, a number of these intelligent spirit beings, when given the choice to follow God or rebel and invent their own plan, chose to rebel from God's rule, and became demons. These evil angels have been partially judged and now test, tempt, and seek to destroy humans from returning to God and His plan for their life.

HEBREWS 1:14

Are they not all ministering spirits, sent out to render service for the sake of those who will inherit salvation?

MATTHEW 18:10

See that you do not despise one of these little ones, for I say to you that their angels in heaven continually see the face of My Father who is in heaven.

EPHESIANS 6:10-12

Finally, be strong in the Lord and in the strength of His might. Put on the full armor of God, so that you will be able to stand firm against the schemes of the devil. For our struggle is not against flesh and blood, but against the rulers, against the powers, against the world forces of this darkness, against the spiritual forces of wickedness in the heavenly places.

8. CHURCH: God has called individual Christians to collect and gather as communities of believers to support one another and be His representatives in the world. These communities of faith are to be His body in the world. Working together, Christians can accomplish seven things that God wants done in the world.

   - **Evangelism**: Spreading the good news about God's forgiveness.

   - **Discipleship**: Learning to live and think as a Christ follower.

   - **Worship**: Exalting God through praise, adoration, and thanksgiving.

   - **Fellowship**: Sharing deep bonds of connectedness with other Christians.

   - **Service**: Serving God by helping our loved ones and others in Christ's power.

   - **Compassion**: Giving tangible evidence of Christ's love to the world.

   - **Generosity**: Showing the world how to live a

generous life with our time, talents, and treasures.

MATTHEW 16:16-19

Simon Peter answered, "You are the Christ, the Son of the living God." And Jesus said to him, "Blessed are you, Simon Barjona, because flesh and blood did not reveal this to you, but My Father who is in heaven. "I also say to you that you are Peter, and upon this rock I will build My church; and the gates of Hades will not overpower it. "I will give you the keys of the kingdom of heaven; and whatever you bind on earth shall have been bound in heaven, and whatever you loose on earth shall have been loosed in heaven."

EPHESIANS 4:11-16

And He gave some as apostles, and some as prophets, and some as evangelists, and some as pastors and teachers, for the equipping of the saints for the work of service, to the building up of the body of Christ; until we all attain to the unity of the faith, and of the knowledge of the Son of God, to a mature man, to the measure of the stature which belongs to the fullness of Christ.

ACTS 2:41-47

So then, those who had received his word were baptized; and that day there were added about three thousand souls. They were continually devoting themselves to the apostles' teaching and to fellowship, to the breaking of bread and to prayer. Everyone kept feeling a sense of awe; and many wonders and signs were taking place through the apostles. And all those who had believed were together and had all things in common; and they began selling their property and possessions and were sharing them with all, as anyone might have need. Day by day continuing with one mind in the temple, and breaking bread from house to house, they were taking their meals together with gladness and sincerity of heart, praising God and having favor with all the people. And the Lord was adding to their number day by day those who were being saved.

9. AFTER-LIFE: God tells us that we will still be alive after our bodies fail. He tells us that we will face a judgment day and then assigned either to a place of love, joy, and peace, or a place of containment for our growing selfishness. God tells us that we will become more and more of what we were becoming here on this earth. If we have chosen to let God teach us the way of love, joy, and peace through Jesus Christ, then He will finish your transformation in that direction and allow you to continue growing in love and service for all eternity. If we have chosen to be self-focused, selfish, and harmful to others, then He will be forced to assign us to that place with others of growing selfishness and evil where we will not do harm to the larger world.

REVELATION 20:11-15

Then I saw a great white throne and Him who sat upon it, from whose presence earth and heaven fled away, and no place was found for them. And I saw the dead, the great and the small, standing before the throne, and books were opened; and another book was opened, which is the book of life; and the dead were judged from the things which were written in the books, according to their deeds. And the sea gave up the dead which were in it, and death and Hades gave up the dead which were in them; and they were judged, every one of them according to their deeds. Then death and Hades were thrown into the lake of fire. This is the second death, the lake of fire. And if anyone's name was not found written in the book of life, he was thrown into the lake of fire.

DANIEL 12:2,3

Many of those who sleep in the dust of the ground will awake, these to everlasting life, but the others to disgrace and everlasting contempt. Those who have insight will shine brightly like the brightness of the expanse of heaven, and those who lead the many to righteousness, like the stars forever and ever.

REVELATION 21:1-27

Then I saw a new heaven and a new earth; for the first heaven and the first earth passed away, and there is no longer any sea. And I saw the holy city, new Jerusalem, coming down out of heaven from God, made ready as a bride adorned for her husband. And I heard a loud voice from the throne, saying, "Behold, the tabernacle of God is among men, and He will dwell among them, and they shall be His people, and God Himself will be among them, and He will wipe away every tear from their eyes; and there will no longer be any death; there will no longer be any mourning, or crying, or pain; the first things have passed away."

REVELATION 22:1-10

Then he showed me a river of the water of life, clear as crystal, coming from the throne of God and of the Lamb, in the middle of its street. On either side of the river was the tree of life, bearing twelve kinds of fruit, yielding its fruit every month; and the leaves of the tree were for the healing of the nations. There will no longer be any curse; and the throne of God and of the Lamb will be in it, and His bond-servants will serve Him; they will see His face, and His name will be on their foreheads. And there will no longer be any night; and they will not have need of the light of a lamp nor the light of the sun, because the Lord God will illumine them; and they will reign forever and ever.

LUKE 16:19-31

Now there was a rich man, and he habitually dressed in purple and fine linen, joyously living in splendor every day. And a poor man named Lazarus was laid at his gate, covered with sores, and longing to be fed with the crumbs which were falling from the rich man's table; besides, even the dogs were coming and licking his sores. Now the poor man died and was carried away by the angels to Abraham's bosom; and the rich man also died and was buried. In Hades he lifted up his eyes, being in torment, and saw Abraham far away and Lazarus in his bosom. And he cried out and said, 'Father Abraham, have mercy on me, and send Lazarus so that he may dip the tip of his finger in water and cool off my tongue, for I am in agony in this flame.' But Abraham said, 'Child, remember that during your life you received your good things, and likewise Lazarus bad things; but now he is being comforted here, and you are in agony. 'And besides all this, between us and you there is a great chasm fixed, so that those who wish to come over from here to you will not be able, and that none may cross over from there to us.' And he said, 'Then I beg you, father, that you send him to my father's house—for I have five brothers—in order that he may warn them, so that they will not also come to this place of torment.' But Abraham said, 'They have Moses and the Prophets; let them hear them.' But he said, 'No, father Abraham, but if someone goes to them from the dead, they will repent!' But he said to him, 'If they do not listen to Moses and the Prophets, they will not be persuaded even if someone rises from the dead.'

2 THESSALONIANS 1:9

These will pay the penalty of eternal destruction, away from the presence of the Lord and from the glory of His power.

10. END TIMES: God tells us that just as Jesus Christ came one time to save the world, He will come again to end history, as we know it. Jesus will come again to usher this world into the future. He will bring justice, truth, and a new world.

MATTHEW 24:29-31

But immediately after the tribulation of those days THE SUN WILL BE DARKENED, AND THE MOON WILL NOT GIVE ITS LIGHT, AND THE STARS WILL FALL *from the sky, and the powers of the heavens will be shaken. And then the sign of the Son of Man will appear in the sky, and then all the tribes of the earth will mourn, and they will see the* Son of Man coming on the clouds of the sky *with power and great glory. And He will send forth His angels with* a great trumpet *and* they will gather together *His elect from the four winds, from one end of the sky to the other.*

1 Thessalonians 4:13-18

But we do not want you to be uninformed, brethren, about those who are asleep, so that you will not grieve as do the rest who have no hope. For if we believe that Jesus died and rose again, even so God will bring with Him those who have fallen asleep in Jesus. For this we say to you by the word of the Lord, that we who are alive and remain until the coming of the Lord, will not precede those who have fallen asleep. For the Lord Himself will descend from heaven with a shout, with the voice of the archangel and with the trumpet of God, and the dead in Christ will rise first. Then we who are alive and remain will be caught up together with them in the clouds to meet the Lord in the air, and so we shall always be with the Lord. Therefore comfort one another with these words.

Revelation 19:11-16

And I saw heaven opened, and behold, a white horse, and He who sat on it is called Faithful and True, and in righteousness He judges and wages war. His eyes are a flame of fire, and on His head are many diadems; and He has a name written on Him which no one knows except Himself. He is clothed with a robe dipped in blood, and His name is called The Word of God. And the armies which are in heaven, clothed in fine linen, white and clean, were following Him on white horses. From His mouth comes a sharp sword, so that with it He may strike down the nations, and He will rule them with a rod of iron; and He treads the wine press of the fierce wrath of God, the Almighty. And on His robe and on His thigh He has a name written, "KING OF KINGS, AND LORD OF LORDS."

How do you react to the above descriptions
of a Christian Worldview?

How do you react to the above descriptions of
Jesus' plan for powerful relationships in your life?

Where do you have questions?

Conclusion

For over 3,000 years, the truths and relational practices of the Judeo-Christian faith have provided the basic structure to understand the world in which we live. A thorough grasp of the basic doctrines and practices of Christianity provide understanding for life and reality. I invite you to drive the truths of Christian teaching deep into your understanding so you will have a framework for understanding the universe, mankind, and life in general. They operate like steel rebar allowing a person to withstand the storms of this life. There are storms because we live in a world gone wrong. Our world is a broken world—broken by the selfish choice of our original parents and broken even further by every other human that came before us.

FOUNDATIONS

BUILDING BLOCK #3

The Wonder of the Church

Building Block #3
The Wonder of the Church

My Story

It has become fashionable these days to criticize the church and point out its flaws. And yes, the church is full of imperfect people trying to follow God's will, and at times the people in the church are selfish and offensive. But I am so grateful to God for the church. I want to take an opportunity to point out what the church uniquely gives every individual and community when it operates even close to healthy; that is, when it is being what God wants it to be.

Let me start by telling you about my family, how Jesus and the church rescued us, and continues to do that to this day. My grandfather on my mother's side of the family was a gambler and a womanizer, who essentially abandoned his family. He would show up occasionally, but for the most part he did not provide for his family. His irresponsibility forced my grandmother and their six children to live in grinding poverty, causing my grandmother to make a series of tragic and even immoral choices in order to put food on the table. The trauma of their choices and the poverty that ensued created all kinds of dysfunction and damage in my mother's family. After years of brokenness, poverty, and dysfunction, my mother became a "wild child," as they described it. After repeated attempts to run away, she was married off to a man to try to control her. His way of control was to beat her and devalue her even more. She eventually ran away from that situation and divorced him.

After a number of years, she met her knight in shining armor, my father, who was dashing, kind, and hardworking. He was also coming from his own broken and dysfunctional family. They decided to get married and start a family. My mother told me that she knew they weren't doing a good job of parenting when my sister's first words were swear words. Was the wreckage of her past going to destroy the future of her children? Her own damage and dysfunction showing up in her children forced her to look for new solutions. My mother saw all of her brothers and sisters trying various things to escape the damage of their past and none of them were really working. She tried the one thing that none of them had tried yet. She went to church and cried out to Jesus to save her and rescue her and her family. Thankfully, she was directed to a Bible-believing church that introduced her to Jesus and began helping her grow in her faith.

Jesus did rescue her and her family. She learned that she was valuable and loved by God at church, even though she had a horrible past. She learned how to parent at church. She learned how to be and stay married at church. Even though my father wanted nothing to do with church in those early days, he did see it helping his wife and kids. The church was making a positive difference in his family, though he believed he didn't need Jesus or the church. He told me years later that when my mother started giving to the church he was against it and was going to stop it. But he began to notice that more money flowed in after she would give, so he figured God must be doing something and didn't say anything. My father saw all the positives that were flowing into his life and family through Jesus and the church and eventually gave his life to Christ years later. The fact that my mother and my father raised us so well and kept the damage from their past out of our lives is a testament to them and to the work of Jesus and the church. I will forever be grateful to what Jesus and the church did for my mother, my father, and our family. My parents and the church did such a good job of raising us that I only recently found out about the full level of brokenness and dysfunction in my mother and father's family. I am so grateful to them, to Jesus, and to the church for giving me a new life with incredible opportunities.

It was not enough to just let Jesus and the church bless me through my family; I needed to embrace Jesus for myself and let the church grow me beyond what I was capable of myself. As I grew up, I discovered that Jesus and the church were offering me what it had done for my mother. When I needed to learn how to become a better version of myself, it was the church that taught me. When I needed to understand how to treat a woman and build a sustainable marriage, it was the church that taught me. When I needed to learn how to parent and raise my children in love, kindness, and responsible behavior, it was the church that taught me. The church taught me how to handle my finances so that they work. The church taught me how to grow in my career; almost every major advancement in my life came through mentors who were a part of the church. Most importantly, the church taught me how to place God at the center of my life and love Him with a whole heart. Without Jesus and the church I would have probably turned back to the failed strategies of my grandfather or others and made a complete mess of my life. I shouldn't have the life I have, and I owe it to my parents, Jesus, and the church.

The churches that I attended were not in any way perfect churches, but they changed my life and my family's life by being faithful to the mission that God gave it. I can point to numerous mentors, classes, and life-changing interactions that all flowed into my life through Jesus and His church. After thirty years of studying the church and helping churches overcome their dysfunction, I am here to tell you about the wonder of the church. You may just be getting started with Jesus and His church, WELCOME. You may have been in church much of your life and yet have not taken full advantage of what God has hidden in the church. Jump in and grow at a Bible-believing church near you. Yes, there will be difficulties at every church, because God fills the churches with imperfect people who are helping each other to pursue God's will, but the church is a gift to the believer and to every local community where it exists. I encourage you to step out in faith and embrace life within whichever church you attend.

What Is the Church and What Does It Contribute?

The church is the creation of God. In His great mercy, He decided to develop, protect, bless, and utilize His people through this unique community of believers who come together as a localized expression of the body of Christ to be God's hands and feet in the world. Changing culture, blessing individuals, rescuing the afflicted, and a hundred other positive things are not possible without this organism called "the church." It is simple and immensely complex all at the same time.

The church is a gift to the world given so that people and communities can overcome the selfishness and evil that resides within them. Yes, I know that it is possible for the church to become corrupt and used as an instrument for evil. There have been numerous examples of churches that were toxic throughout history. But that does not mean we should abandon this wonderful organism that God gave believers and the world. We don't stop having families because some families become corrupt and toxic. We don't stop having government because some governments become corrupt and evil. We don't stop driving cars because some of them are defective or get in accidents. The church, when functioning even close to how it should, is a huge blessing to everyone it is near.

The church is a gift to the believer and to humanity in every local community where it exists. It is a tragedy that the church has not lived up to its incredible calling at various points in the past. It is also a tragedy that major parts of the present culture have been blinded to the wonder of the church because of a few negative expressions of the church. What many don't realize is that hospitals, prison reform, abolition of slavery, hotels, prevention of cruelty to animals, rescue missions, rules for warfare, and recovery groups sprang up out of the church. When functioning the way it should, the church develops individuals and launches them into the world to make difference in God's name.

God gave three institutions to humanity to bring about order and civilized communities: the family, government, and the church. Each one is crucial to the creation of just and orderly societies. When the family functions as it should, there is no better place to rear children and provide stability for men and women throughout the whole of their life. When the government functions properly (without corruption), all the citizens of a community are protected and have access to justice for their issues and causes. When the church functions properly, the believer and the community benefit as the faith and the way of love is explained to more people. The world that we live in is a world where people are allowed to make selfish and even evil choices that impact dozens and even thousands of people around them. The church is a part of God's plan for containing the damage of mankind's corrupt use of limited freedom of the will and also repairing that damage. We do not live in a perfect world and we need all three organizations that God gave in order to survive this brutal world and thrive within it: the family, the government, and the church.

The church is a group of Christians, usually ten or more, who come together to accomplish Jesus Christ's mission in the world. These believers gather by God's power and direction to do things together and for each other that they could not do before they became a church. God works with, through, on, and in a church. A church is not a building, a corporation, or an enterprise. It is an organization, an institution, and an organism that God created to add a series of positive benefits to a society that the other two essential institutions (family and government) can't meet. The Church was planned before the world began (EPHESIANS 1:3) and was discussed during Christ's years of life and ministry on the earth (MATTHEW 16:15). It did not officially begin until the day of Pentecost when the Holy Spirit was given to believers (ACTS 2).

I have spent my whole adult life promoting, repairing, encouraging, correcting, and developing various local expressions of the church. It is the body of Christ in this world until Jesus personally returns. When the church is healthy (not perfect), it accomplishes amazing things that are vitally needed in every society. When the church is doing what it is supposed to do there is hope for people who lack meaning, justice for those who are being oppressed, compassion for those who are afflicted, and direction for those who are lost. The church has made numerous mistakes and ignored significant wrongs in various places in the past, but it has an error-correcting code (the Bible) and error-correcting agents (pastors, prophets, evangelists, apostles and lay people with Bibles) that keep pushing it forward to fulfill its mission.

There is a myth that Christianity and the church has been a plague on society, an evil entity full of oppression and greed. Nothing could be further from the truth. Christianity and the church is a vital organization for the spread of the good news from God. Christians cannot exist alone in a healthy way, so God designed an organism to help support, direct, and protect those who listen to His call to a relationship with Him. I can confidently say that Christianity and the church have been highly beneficial to individuals and the culture at large. Let's look at some major contributions that Christianity and the church have made to mankind:

Historically, Christianity and the church have been a huge benefit to mankind, having started many charitable organizations and promoting changes in society. Christians and churches started many powerful charitable organizations and institutions because they saw a need in society and moved to meet that need. These needs had existed for thousands of years before, but when the Church arrived, these beneficial ministries and developments began to spring up.

- The first hospitals;
- The first homeless shelters;
- The first orphanages;
- The first mental hospitals;
- The first ministry to crime victims;
- The first prison reform ministry;
- The first Society for the Prevention of Cruelty to Animals (SPCA);
- Rescuing females from infanticide;
- Doing away with the veiling of women;
- Abolition of slavery, championed by Christians;
- Promoting equal status of women based upon

GALATIANS 3:28;
- Equal rights because of equality of souls;
- Affecting change to ban Gladiatorial combat (Telemachus);
- Christian missionaries developed over 1,261 written languages for cultures without them.
- Many of the great universities and centers of learning were started by Christians: Harvard, Yale, Princeton, Dartmouth, and more.

Scientifically, Christianity and the church has been a huge benefit to mankind. The following is a list of world famous scientists who are responsible for much of our understanding of our world. They were all Christians who embraced the idea that God made an orderly world that can be understood by humans. It is because of the idea that a rational God would make a rational universe that we have the scientific advancements that we have today.

- Copernicus
- Kepler
- Galileo
- Newton
- Faraday
- Pascal
- Mendel
- Boyle
- Planck
- Descartes
- Leibniz
- Gassendi
- Cuvier
- Lyell
- Joule
- Kelvin
- Ohm
- Pasteur

Christianity's assumption of a reasonable, ordered, knowable universe allowed science to begin. Dinesh DeSouza emphasizes the development of science in a Christian society in his book, *What Is so Great about Christianity?* He writes, "Science as an organized, sustained enterprise arose only once in human history. And where did it arise? In Europe, in the civilization, then called Christendom. Why did modern science develop here and nowhere else? In his September 12, 2006 speech in Regensburg, Germany, Pope Benedict XVI argued that it was due to Christianity's emphasis on the importance of reason."

DeSouza goes on to say about this unique development of science and investigation in Western Civilization, "Philosopher Ernest Fortin writes that while the highest discipline in Judaism and Islam is jurisprudence, the highest discipline in Christianity is theology. The Christian theologian is charged with employing reason to understand the ways of God. There are no theologians in Hinduism or Buddhism because human beings are not called to investigate God's purpose in this manner."

Medically, Christianity and the church have been a huge benefit physically, emotionally, and mentally. These are the proven positive results for those who attend church services regularly. Having looked at numerous studies done at various universities around the world and in the United States, there are appreciable differences between those who attend church services and those that do not.

- Greater physical and mental health;
- Lower rates of drug and alcohol abuse;
- Increased quality of life;
- Enhanced recovery from illness;
- Marital happiness and fewer divorces;

- Happier and more successful children; and
- Increased life expectancy (by 8-13 years).

To cite just one study done in Washington County, Maryland with 91,909 subjects, their conclusion was that the more religiously committed you are, the more likely you are to benefit health-wise:
- 50% reduction in coronary artery disease;
- 56% reduction in emphysema;
- 74% reduction in cirrhosis of the liver;
- 53% reduction in suicides;
- Lower risk and incidence of sexually transmitted diseases;
- Reduced alcohol use; and
- Reduced pulmonary tuberculosis.

One of the more interesting points of the study was one that compared those who smoked and ate fatty foods and went to church and those who smoked and ate fatty foods and didn't go to church. Those who went to church had significantly lower blood pressure than those who did not go to church. (G.W. Comstock and K.B. Partridge, *"Church Attendance and Health," Journal of Chronic Diseases 25, 1972.)*

Interestingly enough, another study conducted at the University of Iowa's Psychology Department showed that regular church attendance contributed significantly to a person's well being. The results were so significant that they recommended doctors prescribe regular church attendance to patients as a prescription for better health.

Socially, Christianity and the church are a huge benefit through their generosity, and have made a huge difference in the world. As a comparison example demonstrating the generosity of Christians to the best efforts culture has to offer, a few years ago the American Idol television show gave 60 million dollars for world hunger, poverty,

AIDS, medical care, etc. This amounted to 30 million dollars per day for two days. This is very commendable. But every year, Christians give 17 billion dollars for world relief and missions over and above what they give to their local churches. This works out to be 50 million dollars every day of every year! God has built into the heart of Christians a generosity of life. One of the church's critics, Nicolas Kristof, who is a writer for the *New York Times* and not a Christian, had this to say about the church's willingness to help make a difference in the world: *"Whenever I show up at a hell hole to help, the Christians are already there helping."*

The body of Christ continues to make a huge difference in our world for good, for God, and for the message of grace. The church has been written off in every age and every culture, and yet it keeps adapting and adjusting like the living organism that it is. How is the church able to add to society and the individual that no other group, institution, or organization adds? God has given the church eight vital functions to collectively and universally move toward accomplishing.

These vital ingredients promote: God's good news of forgiveness, maximum individual development, a positive attitude of thanksgiving and acknowledgement of the Transcendent, the need of community, unleashing compassion, serving others both alike and different, servant leadership, and the development of a generous life.

Eight Vital Ingredients of the Church

1. EVANGELISM. The church is the only institution that is dedicated to spreading the truth about God's plan of forgiveness and restoration, eliminating religion and oppression. Heaven, eternal life, and a relationship with God are free gifts for those who will respond to God's call. Religion is an attempt to earn God's favor by good works or spiritual actions. When the church operates correctly, the church is the only organization that is dedicated to dispelling the myths of religion and helping people understand the amazing offer God makes through Jesus Christ. God declares that through the life, death, and resurrection of Jesus Christ, all of the penalties, judgment, and evil that an individual has done are forgiven. All the person has to do is receive the gift through expressing faith in Jesus Christ as their Savior and God. Religion and superstition are everywhere peddling its oppression and false hope as a way back to God through a person's own effort. Religion and superstition are suppressed when the real church moves forward. The true church of Christ spreads the knowledge of the forgiveness of God and a relationship with God through Jesus' life, death, and resurrection, eliminating the superstition and oppression of religion. Even the enemies of the church proclaimed that they wish there was a God, because God and the church gives what society needs. We call this evangelism.

2. DISCIPLESHIP. The church is the only institution that consistently promotes Christian living and Christian thinking. When it operates correctly, the church develops people in the ten relationships of life so that they can reach their maximum level of love, joy, and peace. The church strips away the

mythology and superstitions that exist in every culture and place, bringing the light of the ten truths into a culture. It is the ten truths of Christian thinking that allow people and a culture to see reality as it really is, rather than remain under the cloud of cultural myths and superstitions. Yes, the church at times has failed to let the ten truths shine into its own myths and superstitions, but it is always open to correction and restructure as God leads it forward. We call this discipleship.

3. WORSHIP. It is this function of reminding people and societies that there is something beyond our lives, our jobs, our cities, and even our planet that is crucial. When individuals and leaders have a self-focused perspective, great evil is possible, because as long as we gain, it doesn't matter who loses. But a weekly reminder of the Transcendence of God draws us out of ourselves to a common, infinite point—God. It is the reminder of the infinite that keeps us from destroying the finite in a rush for personal benefit and pleasure. There is something beyond us; there is something beyond our life; there is someone who is over, above, beyond, and excelling anything we can contemplate. It is the regular reminder of our smallness and His transcendence that is crucial to a functioning society. Every time the Transcendence of God is lost, people do horrible things to one another because they make themselves gods. We call presenting and promoting the Transcendence of God worship.

4. FELLOWSHIP. The church is the only institution that is committed to connecting people of all kinds, types, cultures, classes, vocations, and genders. The church connects people together and roots them in something that is bigger than one's

own self-interest, one's own culture, one's own class distinctions, one's own prejudices, and perspectives. The church connects people through one element—their faith in Jesus Christ as their Lord and Savior. It is this connection through faith that bridges the divides of culture, tradition, gender, and class. The connections that the church universal can make opens eyes to the unity of humanity in ways that is not possible in any other organization. The church mandates loving individuals who share the love of the Savior and extending that love even to those who have not embraced the forgiveness available in Jesus Christ. The church, when it operates as it should, allows people from every tongue, tribe, and people group to push past outward evidence and to examine the heart, the soul of people, and to find a kindred being. This is why members of the church universal have given their lives and wealth for people that are completely different from them. This is why unique cross-cultural, cross-racial, cross-class interactions have occurred in the church to powerfully benefit the world at large. Yes, parts of the local expressions of the church have done a poor job with this component in various parts of the world and at various times in history. But the church that operates correctly moves around these culturally hardened spots and moves forward. We call this fellowship.

5.   UNLEASHING COMPASSION. When the church operates correctly, it introduces powerful change to individuals, society, and culture. It is the distinctively Christian perspective on living that has allowed such radical re-examinations of cultural norms, such as gladiator games, slavery, animal cruelty, gender inequality, racial inequality, the rule of law, and governmental corruption. The church is the only organization

that is dedicated to unleashing compassion, justice, and righteousness worldwide. The church is the number one charitable organization across regions and time. No other organization has had the reach nor the staying power to help the afflicted, the poor, the underprivileged, the oppressed, and the downtrodden. Each local expression of the church focuses on some expressions of these needs and ignoring others. But the church universal is active in every legitimate cause, rescuing, helping, benefiting, and restructuring people, societies, and issues. God activates His body (the people cells of His church) to engage on these issues at tremendous cost. God encourages people to make a tangible difference in the lives of others and He gives those who listen great joy and significance. We live in a world full of mankind's sinful choices and we will not make this world perfect (as God has already designed the next life to be the one that operates perfectly), but we can and will make a significant difference for many and will escape our own self-focus in the process. We call this caring for the afflicted, the poor, the underprivileged, the oppressed, and the downtrodden unleashing compassion.

6. SERVICE. The church is the only worldwide organization that equips its people to discover what unique, special abilities God has placed in them to serve others. God has given every believer at least one special ability when they became Christians. They were provided in order to serve others and sense the power of God flowing through them. The church provides significant opportunities that are not about monetary gain. It helps a person engage a new spiritual power that allows God to flow through a person, affecting others in a positive way. There is something powerful that takes place when we

minister to others using the power of God that flows through us. Christians are equipped on how to live as a Christian and how to think as a Christian so they can serve God in the way that He directs. This need to serve is baked into the life of a true Christian. The church equips people on how to serve others outside of its own organization. It has a certain percentage of people who serve the organization itself, but it also wants to send out its people into the communities and arenas where help is needed. We call this equipping for service. Yes, some local expressions of the church have become self-focused and insulated. However, this is always a self-defeating proposition, and eventually, God's people escape the arbitrary confines of one person's leadership to be released out into the larger world that needs their unique giftedness. We call this service.

7. LEADERSHIP. The church is the only organization where its leadership development strategy is not driven by money, prestige, power, or pleasure. Instead, it is interested in producing life change in individuals, communities, and societies. The leadership development strategy is servant leadership (MATT 20:25-28), and it is love-driven, rather than self-focused and perks driven. Yes, some local expressions of the church have been directed by self-focused individuals, but even their use of leadership of the church has benefited individuals, communities, and societies, because the purpose of the church is not money, power, prestige, or pleasure. Those in leadership in the church are rewarded the more that they help people. The more they serve the people of their region using their unique gifts, talents, and abilities, the more the individuals, the group of believers, and the community benefit. We call this servant leadership.

8. STEWARDSHIP. The church is the only worldwide organization that encourages its members to develop a lifestyle of generosity. A lifestyle of generosity in the area of time, talent (expertise), and treasures is a game changer for people and for communities. How are communities going to end the cycles of poverty and damage that can plague a family for generations? It needs people who will volunteer their time to mentor young people. It needs people who will use their expertise to help people who don't know what they know. It needs people to share some of their resources with those who are less well off. When people become generous, their world changes and all kinds of positive elements begin to occur for them. God has allowed many people to be able to gain money, abilities, and control over their time so that they can be generous with others. It is the sharing of these areas of relative abundance with others that bring much higher levels of significance, joy, and meaning to our lives. We call this lifestyle of generosity stewardship.

Which of these essential elements does your church do well?

Which one of these essential elements is missing or is underdeveloped in the church you attend?

Which one of these essential elements intrigues you the most?

A Vibrant and Healthy Church—How Does a Church Do this Practically?

A healthy church is evidence of God in the world. Many churches have become less than what Christ wants His church to be. If we combat the most common problems that keep the church from reaching more people and training them into fullness in Christ, we can develop a vibrant and healthy church. Here are some practical things a church can do to be all that Christ wants it to be.

Target by Purpose

The purpose of the church is Evangelism, Discipleship, Worship, Fellowship, Service, Compassion, and Stewardship. Everything the church does must aim to accomplish at least one of these purposes. One of the great problems for many churches is that they have a lack of purpose. A dynamic church focuses on accomplishing these purposes. It is easy for a church to begin to focus on other things than these spiritual purposes, but it diminishes the church when this happens. Jesus is clear that this is what He wants His organization to do.

- **Evangelism:** Spreading the good news about God's forgiveness. (MATT 4:19)
- **Discipleship:** Learning to live and think as a Christ follower. (MATT 28:18-20)
- **Worship:** Exalting God through praise, adoration, and thanksgiving. (MATT 4:10)
- **Fellowship:** Sharing deep bonds of connectedness with other Christians. (ACTS 2:42-47)
- **Service:** Serving God by helping Christians and our loved ones in Christ's power. (JOHN 13:34,35)
- **Compassion:** Giving tangible evidence of Christ's love to the

world. (JOHN 13:34,35)

- **Stewardship**: Showing the world how to live a generous life with our time, talents, and treasures. (1 COR. 16:1-3)

Worship as a Celebration of God's Goodness

When the church gathers together, it is to be a celebration of what God has done and is doing. Sincere praise and adoration of God, along with honest prayer, brings a special presence of God into His followers, the church. It is sad that many churches go Sunday after Sunday and never experience a new and special touch from God through worship and coming together. There is something special that happens when the people of God gather together to thank God for the provisions, energy, guidance, opportunities, and miracles of the last week. When people focus on God's wonders and what He has done for them, it recalibrates their lives. It is needed every week. It is easy to become focused on our problems and disappointments. But we will not be able to overcome these unless we spend some time every week reminding ourselves about the blessings of God and the good things of our life.

Engage in Intensive Prayer

The people of God are a powerful force when they petition the Almighty God to act in accordance with His will. It is only through asking God to release His power and glorify His name that the church will significantly advance. The church is God's business and we must ask Him to bless it and exalt Himself in it.

Foster New Relationships

When God's people gather together, they are to be constantly challenged to enter into new relationships in at least two ways:

1. A dynamic church should invite everyone into new relationships with each other as people give, love, and care for one another. God is constantly adding new people to His community of faith. Reach out, get to know them, sit with them at a class, and/or invite them into a small group.

2. Learn how to transform our old relationships by following Jesus' way in them. Each person has ten basic relationships that make up their life. Jesus Christ has a way or plan for each of those basic relationships that will transform those relationships into a whole new quality of life.

Develop a Life-Change Process

God's desire is that every person will become a part of a group of like-minded believers so that they can "grow in the grace and the knowledge of our Lord Jesus Christ." The church must understand how to help people go deeper into God's favor and further into a complete understanding of Jesus Christ. It is a great disappointment when a church does not assist people to become like Christ but only seeks to gather a crowd or tickle ears.

Application Preaching

Sermons should show the power of the Bible in every-day life. There are many truths in the Scripture, but those truths must be related to real life. Boring or irrelevant sermons are a waste of time and border on sin.

Kindness and Acceptance of Everyone

Every person is somewhere on a spiritual journey, whether toward or away from God. Value everyone's own spiritual journey, even if that journey is away from God. Legalism is deadly to the love in a church. We must treat with kindness and acceptance those whom God is drawing to himself.

Every Member a Minister

God has declared that every believer in Christ has been given gifts, talents, and abilities to accomplish His will on His team. It is the pastor's job to get you into the game. God wants you to effectively use your gifts, passion, and abilities to change the world through the individuals you contact, and the choices you make. Nothing deadens a church more than when the pastors are expected to do everything in the church.

Simple Structure

A church is to be a lean, mean organization designed to minister to people for God's name and glory. A church that seeks to keep the layers of structure simple and allow those whom God has called into ministry to be free to minister within reasonable boundaries is dynamic. The church must not create watchdogs or slaves and must fight bureaucracy constantly.

The Discipleship Process

One of the key responsibilities of the church is to turn Christ-followers into disciples, or learners. There are four vital discipleship cycles that a dynamic church plans, directs, and provides for individuals:

1. DAILY discipleship cycle
2. WEEKLY discipleship cycle
3. YEARLY discipleship cycle
4. FIVE-TEN year discipleship cycle.

All of these cycles together are called "discipleship," or learning to follow Jesus Christ. They are vital for the individual believer to have a strong spiritual life. The individual supplies the first discipleship cycle usually with help from the church, the daily cycle, but the church must supply the other three discipleship cycles completely.

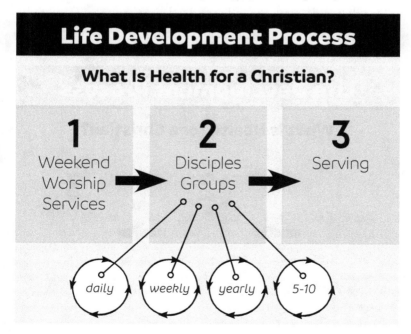

What is the daily discipleship cycle for an individual?

It is the routines, processes, and steps that the individual believer goes through to spend time with God each day. There are many different ways that a believer can do this, but each Christian needs to come to understand how to move his own spiritual formation forward. It could mean spending more time in nature; it could mean less. It could mean more time practicing certain spiritual exercises over other spiritual exercises. In the last class, we recommended the C.H.R.I.S.T. plan for daily devotions as a way to get started in a daily time with God. A great goal is to spend a good hour with God each day.

What is the weekly discipleship cycle that believers need?

When the church is healthy, it takes responsibility to plan and direct a vibrant weekly growth cycle (plan). A basic weekly discipleship cycle is W.W.L.S. or Worship, Witness, Learning, and Service. This means that every week the individual believers are encouraged to be worshippers, witnesses, disciples, and servants.

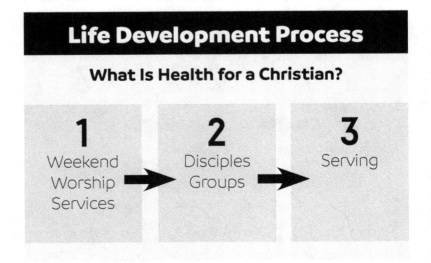

There is something vital about the corporate nature of most of these weekly growth elements. When we engage with others in the learning and practicing of our faith, the impact is deeper and longer lasting.

What is the yearly discipleship cycle that believers need?
The church that is helping its people the most has a life development plan for them that will not let them be at the same spiritual level year after year. The healthy church has a 5-10 year plan for transformational experiences in all the topics of Orthopraxy and Orthodoxy. It is important for the church not to teach fads or ear-tickling topics, but to cover the whole counsel of God over some time period.

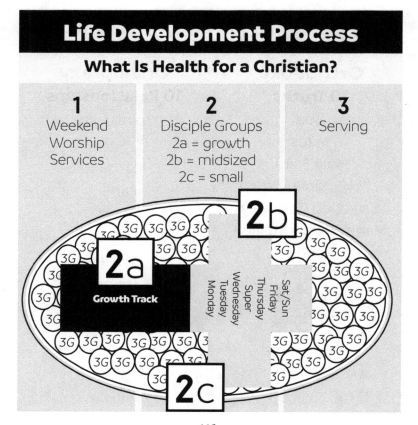

Life Development Process

What Is Health for a Christian?

1	2	3
Weekend Worship Services	Disciple Groups 2a = growth 2b = midsized 2c = small	Serving

If a person stays in a church through one of their life stages, will they be offered a transformative experience around the teaching of the Bible about loving God, about personal development, about marriage, about family, about work, about money, about friends, about church, about society and about enemies? They must come to understand in a foundational and/or deeper way the Christian truths about God, about Jesus Christ, about the Holy Spirit, about the Bible, about salvation, about the church, about angels (good and evil), about the afterlife, and about the return of Christ to wrap up history.

Discipleship

Orthodoxy 10 Truths	Orthopraxy 10 Relationships
God	Spirituality
Jesus	Self
Holy Spirit	Marriage
Bible	Family
Salvation (Success)	Work
Mankind (Spirituality)	Church
Angels	Money
Church	Friends
After Life	Community
End Times	Enemies

Conclusion

The church is the only organization that is committed to presenting and praising the Transcendence of God. It provides a sense of transcendence and design to our lives and the world. Understanding the existence of God and collectively praising the super intellect behind the Universe changes people in significant ways. Christ's church promotes transcendence, hope, and a positive outlook on life, and it contributes significantly into the lives of individuals and communities. When one contemplates the fact of an Almighty God, and His investment into the creation and continued sustenance of His body, the Church, one has hope in the midst of the tribulation of this world.

FOUNDATIONS

BUILDING BLOCK #4

Finding and Living in the Will of God

Building Block #4
Finding and Living in the Will of God

Every person on this planet has an innate desire to feel significant and to live lives of meaning. That is because God designed each person that way, with a destiny that only they can fulfill. A meaningful life always revolves around living in the will of God. It is best experienced through wise, Christian decisions that fill our lives with love and explore the unique combination of who we are, our unique experiences, and our unique opportunities. Wise decisions about an opportunity that is offered, a talent that is needed, and a developing gift are all invitations to a meaningful life (EPH. 5:15). The question is whether the individual will understand and grasp the opportunities and recognize the path to a meaningful life when it is offered.

Moses was out tending sheep one day when he was 80 years of age. He saw a bush catch fire, but it did not burn up. If Moses had not turned aside to check out the bizarre phenomena of the burning bush, he would have missed his chance for a meaningful life and most likely, his life would have been lost to history (Ex. 2-3). We all have interesting opportunities offered to us, and ideas that prompt our minds. Which ones should we explore? Which ones will lead to a great life? Which ones are God's will? That is what we will explore in this chapter.

The Bible tells us that God has a wonderful plan for our life (EPH. 2:10). His plan maximizes who we are and pushes us to levels and expressions that we may not attain on our own. He has good works that He has planned for us to do. He has made us and shaped us to accomplish crucial things for our benefit, other's blessing, and His overall purposes. When we live in His will, our life glows with meaning and significance. To be in God's will means that we actively participate in the good works that He sends our way. These are good works that we are uniquely equipped to accomplish. We were put here for a reason and we are still alive to accomplish key things. When our purpose is done then God is free to call us home to heaven.

Many people have mistakenly embraced the idea that life is really all about them. Unfortunately, a number of people live their life pushing their self-focused agenda on others. The Bible calls this self-focused life foolishness. You may gain all you want but lose your soul in the process. Many people believe that if they get everything they want then they will have a meaningful life. But it is clear that this is not true. We have all read about or known someone who had almost everything they wanted but were miserable. It is almost counter-intuitive that life becomes meaningful when we make a significant contribution to others and we align our life with God and His purposes for our life. Jesus said that the greatest commandments that fulfill all that God wants from us is to love God and to love others as we righteously love ourselves (MATT. 22:37,38).

How Do I Find God's Will?

A meaningful life is about filling our lives with loving relationships. God's will always includes making a positive contribution into other people's lives. We could think of God's will as being a combination of wise decisions, love, and the uniqueness of the individual. Of all the things we can do and all the people we can spend time with, ask yourself:

- How do I make wise decisions?
- How do I fill my life with righteous love?
- How do I know how I am supposed to make a loving contribution to society?

Learning to Make a Wise Decision

Living in the will of God has some known boundaries and signposts. We want to work our way through seven markers that always appear in the will of God. If you work your way through this short list, you can have a pretty good idea if something is in the will of God for you. When we have an opportunity to do something or enter into a relationship, it is important to run whatever or whoever it is through these crucial check points to see if it is within the will of God.

Read Scripture

Does what I am contemplating agree with Scripture, or does it cause me to violate Scripture? Christians understand that the Scriptures provide the basic rules for life. So if what a person wants to do violates Scripture, then it can't be the right decision. On the other hand, if what the person wants to do is encouraged and applauded in Scripture, then it most likely is the will of God.

Look at what the Bible says about the truths that it contains.

> *"All Scripture is inspired by God and profitable for teaching, for reproof, for correction, for training in righteousness; so that the man of God may be adequate, equipped for every good work."*
>
> (2 TIM. 3:16-17)

> *"The law of the LORD is perfect, restoring the soul; The testimony of the LORD is sure, making wise the simple. The precepts of the LORD are right, rejoicing the heart; The commandment of the LORD is pure, enlightening the eyes. The fear of the LORD is clean, enduring forever; The judgments of the LORD are true; they are righteous altogether. They are more desirable than gold, yes, than much fine gold; Sweeter also than honey and the drippings of the honeycomb. Moreover, by them Your servant is warned; In keeping them there is great reward."*
>
> (PSALM 19:7-11)

A short hand way of embracing all the ideas of Scripture is to think of these categories, "good vs. evil," "love vs. harm," or "righteousness vs. wickedness." Does the idea, action, or activity promote good, love, or righteousness? Or does it require me or others to do evil, harm others, or do wickedness? (ROM 2:7) If an action or an opportunity promotes good, love, and righteousness, then it will benefit God, others, and myself all at the same time and over the long haul. Righteous is what is *right* for all parties concerned. The will of God will always be right, good, and beneficial to God, others, and myself. The will of God may be (and sometimes should be) oppositional to those who are promoting evil. It is proper to say that the will of God causes benefit, blessing, and progress for people of good will.

Another way of understanding this biblical promotion of righteousness is to look at the negative side. Does the activity, opportunity, action, or idea require a violation of the moral boundaries of the Ten Commandments? If it does, then it can't be the will of God. The Ten Commandments are God's shorthand version of actions and ideas that will immediately or eventually harm others. God is saying that beyond these boundary lines is destruction and damage.

We will all get ideas or promptings of ways to profit or move forward that require us to go outside of these moral boundaries for some period of time. If that is what is required, then the idea or activity can't be the will of God. Let's look at the helpful boundaries that are in the Ten Commandments. (Ex. 21:3-17)

Here is an abbreviated version of them:

You shall have no other gods before me.

You shall not make any graven images.

You shall not take the name of the Lord your God in vain.

Remember the Sabbath day to keep it holy.

Honor your Father and your Mother.

You shall not murder.

You shall not commit adultery.

You shall not steal.

You shall not bear false witness against your neighbor.

You shall not covet anything that belongs to your neighbor.

In this next section, I have asked the relevant question about each commandment to see if what a person wants to do would violate the commandment or stay within its boundaries. I have also provided a diagram below to illustrate this idea. Notice that the will of God is not always a straight line. There will be bends in the road of life, but there will always be boundary lines to stay within made up of the Ten Commandments.

Think of them like the border of a sidewalk. When your actions or decisions take you off of the sidewalk, you are outside the permissive will of God.

1. Will I or other people be required to put something else ahead of God?

2. Will I or other people be required to misrepresent God or worship a different god?

3. Will I or other people need to swear, curse, or denigrate God or righteous living?

4. Will I or other people need to move beyond work, rest, and spiritual balance in life?

5. Will I or other people need to rebel from righteous authorities?

6. Will I or other people need to use anger, violence, or the threat of violence?

7. Will I or other people need to be sexually promiscuous or unfaithful?

8. Will I or other people need to steal?

9. Will I or other people need to lie or deceive others?

10. Will I or other people need or want to take what is rightfully another's possession?

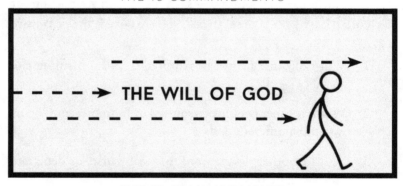

Pray

As you pray and contemplate doing the activity, idea, action, or opportunity, do you have peace and encouragement from God along this line? We also should pray and ask God for clarity about whether we should do a particular thing we are thinking about. Some of our opportunities may be temptations. Some of our ideas will be wonderful, God-given opportunities to advance love, righteousness, and joy. Many times all of these come disguised as problems and difficulties. God wants us to grapple with Him on which ones to move forward with and which ones to walk away from. If the Scriptures are clear that we should not do something, then we don't need to pray about an idea that requires us to steal something. But most of our opportunities are not that clear cut. Prayer for direction, clarity, and guidance is very helpful. We do need to recognize that we are probably biased toward wanting to do something, so our sense of God's answer may be unclear.

Usually I recommend that we tell God what we would like to see happen, but let Him make it clear if the answer is either "yes" or "no," or some modification. I follow Philippians 4:6-8 on this. Let God know everything you want to say about your possibility. Let Him know that you give Him the right to say "No." You just want clarity.

> *"Be anxious for nothing, but in everything by prayer and supplication with thanksgiving let your requests be made known to God. And the peace of God, which surpasses all comprehension, will guard your hearts and your minds in Christ Jesus."* (PHIL 4:6,7)

> *"But I say, walk by the Spirit, and you will not carry out the desire of the flesh."* (GAL. 5:16)

"They passed through the Phrygian and Galatian region, having been forbidden by the Holy Spirit to speak the word in Asia; and after they came to Mysia, they were trying to go into Bithynia, and the Spirit of Jesus did not permit them; and passing by Mysia, they came down to Troas." (ACTS 16:6-8)

Check in with Authorities

One of the often-overlooked areas to receive clarity about a decision is check with the appropriate authority already in your life. What do your appropriate authorities think about this idea, activity, opportunity, or action? I am amazed that we often ignore this incredible source of wisdom because they could "order" us to not do it. God has placed authorities in various parts of our life so that we cannot do anything we want. Sometimes we don't want to ask our authorities because they could say "No." We often only want to talk with people who are most likely to say "Yes." But "No" is an answer and I often find that a reasonable authority asks great questions and can modify an idea in a wonderful way to make it more successful.

Fill your authority in on what you are thinking, and you will be surprised at how much smarter your decisions will start to be. If the appropriate authority cares about you and will listen to what you think, then you want to get their wisdom and expertise.

"Every person is to be in subjection to the governing authorities. For there is no authority except from God, and those which exist are established by God. Therefore whoever resists authority has opposed the ordinance of God; and they who have opposed will receive condemnation

upon themselves. For rulers are not a cause of fear for good behavior, but for evil. Do you want to have no fear of authority? Do what is good and you will have praise from the same;" (ROM. 13:1-3)

Seek Wise Counsel

Another great place to get wisdom regarding an opportunity or idea is from wise Christians who have been successful with a similar venture. Too often when we are evaluating an idea we want people to be as excited as we are and so we only ask people who we think will be excited with us right from the start. But sharp, experienced, and knowledgeable people will be able to see the pitfalls and the crucial steps that will make an idea successful. Wise people ask questions to see how deeply we understand what is really involved in making an idea work.

What do wise Christians think about this idea, opportunity, action, or activity? Someone else has done almost everything we want to do successfully before. It is very helpful to get their opinions and advice on what you are thinking. The insights and encouragement that these successful people give will help you decide whether it is the wise thing to do for you.

> *"Therefore if there is any encouragement in Christ, if there is any consolation of love, if there is any fellowship of the Spirit, if any affection and compassion, make my joy complete by being of the same mind, maintaining the same love, united in spirit, intent on one purpose. Do nothing from selfishness or empty conceit, but with humility of mind regard one another as more important*

than yourselves; do not merely look out for your own personal interests, but also for the interests of others." (PHIL. 2:1-3)

"And He gave some as apostles, and some as prophets, and some as evangelists, and some as pastors and teachers, for the equipping of the saints for the work of service, to the building up of the body of Christ; until we all attain to the unity of the faith, and of the knowledge of the Son of God, to a mature man, to the measure of the stature which belongs to the fullness of Christ. As a result, we are no longer to be children, tossed here and there by waves and carried about by every wind of doctrine, by the trickery of men, by craftiness in deceitful scheming; but speaking the truth in love, we are to grow up in all aspects into Him who is the head, even Christ,..." (EPH. 4:11-15)

Use Common Sense

There are many things that we want to try but they really don't make sense. They may just be a wild idea that passed through our mind. Does this idea, activity, opportunity, or action make sense in some way? Yes, there are outside-the-box thoughts and plans, but they will have some grounding in reality. Just because you thought about something or just because an idea came through your head doesn't mean it is God's will. It must make sense in some way.

I have known a lot of people who want to do something so badly that they do not evaluate whether this is good for them, good for the other person, or good for society. They are blinded by their own want. The idea just doesn't make sense but they don't want to think about the lunacy of the idea. They just know that they want to give it a try. Unfortunately many people attach their want, passion, or interest to God, "This must be from God." Not necessarily! It may just be your subjective desire masquerading as being from God.

"Therefore be careful how you walk, not as unwise men but as wise,..." (EPH. 5:15)

"But the Spirit explicitly says that in later times some will fall away from the faith, paying attention to deceitful spirits and doctrines of demons, by means of the hypocrisy of liars seared in their own conscience as with a branding iron,..." (1 TIM. 4:1,2)

"And just as they did not see fit to acknowledge God any longer, God gave them over to a depraved mind, to do those things which are not proper, being filled with all unrighteousness, wickedness, greed, evil; full of envy, murder, strife, deceit, malice; they are gossips, slanderers, haters of God, insolent, arrogant, boastful, inventors of evil, disobedient to parents, without understanding, untrustworthy, unloving, unmerciful; and although they know the ordinance of God, that those who practice such things are worthy of death, they not only do the same, but also give hearty approval to those who practice them." (ROM. 1:28-32)

Pay Attention to Open Doors

If God is in something, then there will be open doors to accomplish it when you begin pushing in that direction. Does this direction have the open doors that are needed to move it forward? There may be opposition from some people but God's will comes with encouragement and open doors to help you know that you should move in this direction. If you have prayed and asked others for advice, but the doors do not open, then accept that it may not be God's will to do something at that time or in that way.

> *"I do not want you to be unaware, brethren, that often I have planned to come to you (and have been prevented so far) so that I may obtain some fruit among you also, even as among the rest of the Gentiles."* (ROM. 1:13)

> *"...for a wide door for effective service has opened to me, and there are many adversaries."* (1 COR. 16:9)

> *"Now when I came to Troas for the gospel of Christ and when a door was opened for me in the Lord,..."*
> (2 COR. 12:2)

> *"I know your deeds. Behold, I have put before you an open door which no one can shut, because you have a little power, and have kept My word, and have not denied My name."* (REV. 3:8)

Look for Provisions

If God is in something, then His resources and provisions will also be provided along the way. Do I have the resources and provisions that are needed to get this done? One of the ways that God says "No" is by withholding resources. It may be a great idea, but it is the wrong time. It may be a great idea, but you are not the right person. God can say "No," and withholding resources is one way to signal it. On the other hand, God saying "Yes" is signaled by Him providing the resources that is needed.

> "...for I know that this will turn out for my deliverance through your prayers and the provision of the Spirit of Jesus Christ,..." (PHIL. 1:19)

> "For this reason I have often been prevented from coming to you; but now, with no further place for me in these regions, and since I have had for many years a longing to come to you whenever I go to Spain—for I hope to see you in passing, and to be helped on my way there by you, when I have first enjoyed your company for a while—..." (ROM. 15:22-24)

When I am trying to make a decision that I am unsure of what God wants, then I run it through the grid and look for green lights.

Scripture   *Prayer*

Authorities   *Wise Christians*

Common Sense   *Open Doors*

Provisions

God's will comes with green lights on each of these. I want all of these areas to be green lights. I am willing to be unclear about the second aspect of prayer (because I may be too close to hear God clearly), but I want all of these aspects of a wise decision to be encouraging me to move forward. Too often we only look at whether we want to do something and we impulsively dash in before we should.

Filling Our Lives with Love

Having walked through these elements of a wise decision, it is time to take into account the second aspect of living in the will of God—fill our life with Love and its many characteristics. The Christian definition of success is a life filled with love in the major relationships of life. Jesus says that the will of God is to fill our lives with love for Him, love for others, and righteous love for ourselves.

> *"And He said to him,* " 'YOU SHALL LOVE THE LORD YOUR GOD WITH ALL YOUR HEART, AND WITH ALL YOUR SOUL, AND WITH ALL YOUR MIND.' *"This is the great and foremost commandment.* *"The second is like it,* 'YOU SHALL LOVE YOUR NEIGHBOR AS YOURSELF.' *"On these two commandments depend the whole Law and the Prophets."* (MATT. 22:37-40)

We have already talked about how becoming a follower of Christ means that we learn how to live as a Christian. This means that we look at filling the relationships of our life with love...Jesus' way. When we start following Jesus, we move from being the "god" of our own life to living life Jesus' way. We have often thought that the way to be supremely happy and successful is to plow forward to do what we want. But Jesus tells us that when we truly learn to love God, others, and ourselves in a righteous manner, our lives are fuller and more meaningful than anything we could accomplish when we were selfishly pursuing our own desire.

We have to understand what love is from a Christian understanding. Love means to meet needs, pursue, and please in that order. If a person has a need and I meet that need, then I have loved them. If a person has a need, a real need, and I ignore the need but greet them pleasantly, I have not truly loved them. My role as a Christian is to meet the needs, pursue, and please the people in my life. I arrange my life so that I can meet the needs of the people in my life. It is this type of life that brings the life of meaning and significance.

Loving God is unique in that He has no needs that I can meet, so my primary way of loving Him is to pursue Him and to please Him. If I am to have a life of meaning and purpose, then I must pursue God and please Him every day. My pursuit of God may not take the highest amount of my time directly, but it is what is behind everything that I do. All of the love that I pour into the other relationships of life grows out of my pursuit of and desire to please God.

Being a Christian means being alert to the whispers of the Holy Spirit to express love. We know what the Holy Spirit will whisper to us because we know what the Fruit of the Spirit is: Love, Joy, Peace, Patience, Kindness, Goodness, Gentleness, Faithfulness, and Self-Control. So the Christian is prepared to have a random thought come across their mind to do something that would bless others, or to say something complimentary to the person at work. To smile at people in the line you're standing in. To say something that will calm the fight. To be willing to wait longer for a change. To be pleasant rather than reactive or angry. To do something that benefits the other person. To yield your rights to the other person even though you could claim them. To stay faithful even though the other person is giving you reason to break the friendship or contract. To stay controlled or disciplined when you don't want to.

Living the Christian life is a wonderful dance with God as He leads us to do things we would not do on our own, but are wonderful evidences of His presence in our life. We are not perfect, but others see God when we listen and respond to the whispers of the Holy Spirit. Listen for His Spirit's prompting and move in His power to do these even though it may not be the way you are feeling at the moment.

The following diagram shows how to move along in life while listening to the Holy Spirit and loving others as you stay within the boundaries of the Ten Commandments.

NOT PERMITTED BY GOD
PERMISSIVE WILL OF GOD

THE 10 COMMANDMENTS

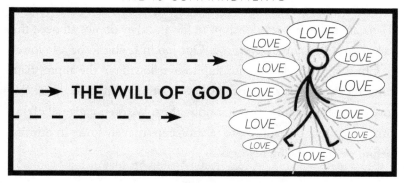

THE 10 COMMANDMENTS

PERMISSIVE WILL OF GOD
NOT PERMITTED BY GOD

Let's talk about another aspect of love that is often overlooked in our day. There is a priority to loving others. Some people deserve more time and attention than other people. Our culture has lost this and often just responds to the loudest or most attractive. God clearly tells us that we should meet certain people's needs before other people's needs. In 1 TIMOTHY 3:1-10, God tells us that a person is not ready to be a leader in the church unless he has adequately loved his spouse and family.

In other words, loving people in the church from a leadership position comes only after one has adequately loved one's family. This is important because I consistently see people put more time, attention, and energy into work, friendships, hobbies, and such, who then wonder why their life is not working.

There are ten major relationships in life and they do not all need the same types and amounts of love. Our job in trying to be a follower of Christ is to fill each relationship to overflowing in the appropriate time and way. Our relationships have a priority order to them. We love the ones that are higher in priority first. We do not give all of our time, attention, or resources to relationships that are lower in priority before we meet the higher ones.

I like to think of my life as a fountain and the people in my life as the basins that catch the water (love) that flow from my time, energy, and resources. The basins (people at the top) receive my love first and then they over flow into the other basins (people).

This is the way that typically the relationships are arranged in priority order in Scripture:

GOD
(pursuing and pleasing Him)

SELF
*(meeting your righteous needs, pursuing your
soul & righteous levels of pleasure)*

MARRIAGE
(meeting needs, pursuing & pleasing our spouse)

FAMILY
(meeting needs, pursuing & pleasing our immediate family)

WORK
*(meeting needs, pursuing & pleasing our bosses, colleagues,
and subordinates)*

CHURCH
*(meeting needs, pursuing & pleasing our Christian
brothers and sisters)*

FINANCES
(making sure money or possessions does not become a god)

FRIENDS
(meeting needs, pursuing & pleasing our friends)

COMMUNITY
(unleashing compassion through real love)

ENEMIES
*(turning our enemies into friends, if possible, through
righteous love)*

Understanding Your S.H.A.P.E. as a Part of God's Will

A third aspect of discerning the will of God for our lives is weighing how the idea, opportunity, or activity lines up with who God made you to be. God has made each of us unique in our gifts, talents, experiences, and opportunities. He wants to use all of these things to shape us into a person that can make a difference in our world. Each of these unique elements leads us to the next arena of His will for us. One of the ways we determine His will for our lives is to look at who He has made us to be. If computers fascinate you, then He most likely wants you to head in that direction. If you have an eye for color and good hand/eye coordination, then He may want us to use that as a surgeon or an artist. If we have experienced sickness or poverty, He wants to use all that you learned to propel you forward.

All the unique things that we can do that others may find difficult and experiences that have happened to us are clues to the ways that God has fitted us to make an impact in the world. Yes, there are times when God has us doing things we may not like or are not suited for (He asks us to walk on water), but the majority of the time He will use us in the areas that we are gifted, talented, and experienced. Most of the time if we are being asked to do something that is truly not us, then it is not God's will.

Each person is a specially designed tool for the glory of God, the advancement of His church, the welfare of the society and their family, and the satisfaction of the individual. Scripture tells us that God has given us five different areas of our life that are clues of how He wants to use us and fulfill us.

These can be summarized using the S.H.A.P.E. acronym. (Pastor Rick Warren was the first person to use this acronym that I am aware of.)

S – Spiritual Gifts
H – Heart
A – Ability
P – Personality
E – Experience

After you have discovered your particular SHAPE and you begin to live using that particular shape you will find your Christian walk much more enjoyable. What you are supposed to do in life is different than what other people should do. God has made each of us unique. In this aspect of God's will, God wants us to be doing that which clearly flows from us and through us. God's will is not what you would hate or what you can't do well (even though there may be times of difficulty and training). His will flows through us and is a blessing to others as we live in it. Realize the will of God is our best path through this life, making the biggest righteous impact.

If we make wise decisions rather than foolish (self-focused) ones, our lives will get better and more productive (as long as evil people are not in charge). If we reorganize our lives to give real love (meeting needs, pursuing, and pleasing) to the people in our lives in priority order, our lives will get significantly better (as long as selfish, evil people are not in charge). Finally, if we understand and act in ways that fit our unique S.H.A.P.E., our lives will get better (as long as evil people are not in charge).

Let's understand God's S.H.A.P.E. for you. We believe that God has been at work in you since before you were born to prepare you for His purposes. (Psa. 139:13-16) We also believe that God has prepared certain good works for you to perform. All that you are made of is required to fulfill God's purposes for you. The various educational courses and any God-given gifts make you a unique agent in God's army. We believe that you will only find fulfillment and satisfaction when you are being properly used by God.

S = Spiritual Gifts

We believe that God has given each Christian at least one spiritual gift (1 Cor. 12:7) to serve His church and impact the world. When a person becomes a Christian, God gives every Christian a spiritual enablement that can help Christians, the church, and/or the world. This spiritual gift is a way that the power of the Holy Spirit flows through us. It is not designed to make us feel better but to minister to others. As we grow in our faith, we become more sensitive to promptings to help in particular ways. These are often the spiritual gift(s) we have been given. We believe that all the scriptural gifts are still available to the Church through God the Holy Spirit's sovereign choice. All the gifts are to strengthen and build up the body of Christ. And they are all to be used decently and in order. Each Christian is to discover the special ability they have been given and employ it to the glory of God. As you grow in the Christian faith, you will begin to notice these spiritual gifts or abilities showing up. Notice them and develop them, as God wants to strengthen other Christians through your use of these gifts. Don't worry if you can't determine what your spiritual gift(s) are right away. They may take a while to begin showing up in the way you follow the Lord Jesus. Focus on the Fruit of the Spirit: Love, Joy, Peace, Patience, Kindness, Gentleness, Faithfulness, and Self-control, and the new spiritual enablements will begin to prompt you.

How to Determine Your Spiritual Gift(s)

Before beginning the process of identifying your potential spiritual gifts, make sure that you are a Christian and are growing in your faith. God gives these special grace gifts to Christians, and they become more manifested the stronger we grow in our faith. Becoming a Christian means accepting Jesus Christ as the Savior from your sins and gives Him full permission to rule your life. Growing in your faith means following the Lord Jesus in the way you live and think.

Step 1: Read over the list of gifts as listed in **Appendix 2**

Step 2: Circle the spiritual gifts that:
a) Seem interesting;
b) You think you have used or are regularly prompted to do;
c) You might have but are yet undeveloped.

Step 3: Practice using a particular gift as you are prompted to do so, or as they are needed in your church.

Step 4: Take the *Spiritual Gifts Test* as found online at ptlb.com.

Step 5: Bring your ideas, answers, and questions to your instructor after class. Look over the various gifts mentioned in **Appendix 2** and you will find some that match the type of promptings that you have been receiving. *See **Appendix 3** for answers to some of your potential questions.*

Step 6: Begin utilizing your spiritual gifts in different ministries. One of your spiritual gifts may be stronger than the other ones. Allow God to flow through you using the gifts that are needed at that moment. One of your spiritual gifts may be stronger or more needed at a particular time in your life. God may need you to exercise one of your gifts in a particular setting.

Step 7: Continue developing and perfecting the use of your spiritual gifts in various situations and opportunities for the rest of your life. There is a growth curve in the understanding and use of spiritual gifts and you can get better at using a spiritual gift. Understanding and using the gifts can become the key to unlocking your future.

H = Heart

We believe that God has placed desires in our heart (Psa. 37:1-4) to serve in certain places (at home, in the church, in a foreign land, in a disadvantaged area, in affluent areas), with certain groups (preschoolers, toddlers, infants, school-age children, youth, singles, retirees, parents, widows, newly married, specially challenged, gifted, young adults, middle-age adults, or the elderly), and in certain capacities (speaking roles, support roles, administrative roles). These become passions. Many times God uses these passions to show us where we need to serve in the church and/or the larger world. If God breaks your heart for a particular cause or problem then push into that area to see if He is leading you in that direction. Even though you may serve at times in a place that is not your passion in ministry, you will serve best and with the most ease and enjoyment when you are ministering in the area of your passion. *See **Appendix 4** for more about passions and developing your God-given dream.*

A = Abilities

We know that God has given every person natural, talents, gifts, and abilities. (Psa. 139:13-16; Ex. 4:10) These natural abilities also help determine where you should serve God. Only rarely does God move in a completely different way against your natural abilities.

Facts about Your Abilities

1. God has given you certain abilities and withheld certain abilities. (Psalms 139:13-16; Ex. 4:10,11)
2. Most career counselors tell us that each person has between 500-700 different abilities.
3. If you don't use your abilities, you may lose the ability to use them well.
4. A large vocabulary helps develop your abilities and allows others to notice and reward your abilities.
5. Unused abilities will begin to "demand" to be used later in life.
6. You will be frustrated if you are doing a job that demands a skill you don't have.

*Also see **Appendix 5** and **Appendix 6** for more about abilities.*

P = Personality

God has given each person a unique blend of temperaments and personality. These different parts of our personality are not there by accident but represent the pre-planning of God. (Psa. 139:13-16) As we understand, accept, and in some cases overcome aspects of our personality, we will be suited for God's job for us.

There are many different ways of measuring and labeling various internal impulses that become regular parts of how we interact with the world around us. These are called personality traits. Some people are prompted to be noticed by others. Some people are prompted to be in charge. Some people are prompted to fit in and make peace. Some people are prompted to get things right and hold to a high standard. Using a different measuring system, some people gain energy by being with people and others get energy by being alone. Some relate to concrete physical objects better and others relate to abstract ideas and nuanced communication. Some prefer making decisions by getting all the facts and being as dispassionate as possible before making a decision, while others prefer to be aware of all the relational and personal factors that are involved in a particular decision. Some enjoy closure and others enjoy keeping their options open. All of these and many others are aspects of personality. God has woven you together to prefer particular promptings and to ignore other ones. This is a part of what makes you the special person you are.

E = Experiences

People are also a bundle of personal experiences, which shape them and help determine where, with whom, and in what capacity they should live their life. The experiences that have barged into our lives and the ones that we have invited to come in, all affect who we are. God may not have chosen all of the ones that are not a part of your permanent memory banks, but He does want to use them to help you build a great life. (Rom 8:28) As we look at the experiences that we have had, we often get a glimpse of where God might be leading us. Take some time to think through the questions below and pray for God to show you the link or commonalities between them. They can provide clues to what you should be doing and whom you should be doing it for.

Look at the significant experiences you have had in your life.

1.

2.

3.

4.

Look at the significant relationships you have had in your life.

1.

2.

3.

4.

Look at the significant organizations that have been a part of your life.

1.

2.

3.

4.

Look at the significant traumas that you have had in your life.

1.

2.

3.

4.

Major Reasons Why People Do Not Pursue God's Will to the Fullest

Fear

Fear holds so many people back from expressing who they really are and what they can really do. God's will seems like a different place but it is the place where a person can be their righteous self. The expression of who we are within the boundaries of goodness and love is a wonderful place. Too often we have been afraid to pursue the deepest expressions of love. We have been tempted to pursue our selfish ideas. These seem easier but they end in poverty of spirit and calamity. It is time to abandon ourselves to the will of God and live in and through His love of us and His love of others.

> *"We have come to know and have believed the love which God has for us. God is love, and the one who abides in love abides in God, and God abides in him. By this, love is perfected with us, so that we may have confidence in the day of judgment; because as He is, so also are we in this world. There is no fear in love; but perfect love casts out fear, because fear involves punishment, and the one who fears is not perfected in love. We love, because He first loved us. If someone says, "I love God," and hates his brother, he is a liar; for the one who does not love his brother whom he has seen, cannot love God whom he has not seen. And this commandment we have from Him, that the one who loves God should love his brother also."* (1 JOHN 4:16-21)

Need for Security

Sometimes we do not completely understand that God can be trusted when He prompts us to move in a particular direction. We become overly concerned about financial issues that are involved in following God. God can be trusted to take care of His children. He has given us a plan to follow financially in the Scriptures that is prudent but involves trusting Him as we live our lives.

Sometimes we wrap up our emotional security in a person or a place or an institution and we are unwilling to let God move us past those emotional touchstones. God can be trusted and at times He needs to help us confront how much of our security is tied to a person, a place, or an institution. Don't be impulsive but if God is calling you to move beyond a particular person, place, or institution, then follow His righteous leading,

It is possible in our day in ways that has not been true in the past to demand a level of physical safety that is unheard of down through history. If we demand that God only take us to places where there is absolute physical safety, then we will never move. Sometimes the very place He wants to send us is not safe and we are supposed to make it safer. Do not miss the will of God just because it might be "unsafe." A missionary friend reminded me years ago, "The safest place to be is in the center of God's will, and the most dangerous place to be is out of the will of God."

> *"Do not love the world nor the things in the world. If anyone loves the world, the love of the Father is not in him. For all that is in the world, the lust of the flesh and the lust of the eyes and the boastful pride of life, is not from the Father, but is from the world. The world is passing away, and also its lusts; but the one who does the will of God lives forever. Children, it is the last hour; and just as you heard that antichrist is coming, even now many*

antichrists have appeared; from this we know that it is the last hour." (1 JOHN 2:15-18)

Lack of Preparation

There are times when God is preparing us for good works that He will bring across our path in the future. Get ready mentally, spiritually, emotionally, relationally, and financially to be used by God in the lives of others. This obviously starts with family and extends out to those whom God puts in your life through work, church, and community.

Most of us are in a period of preparation for the good works that are to come. Don't miss out on what God has in store because you didn't want to go to school or learn a skill or interact with a difficult person. A whole world of significance and impact is waiting just beyond the preparation you are doing.

> *"How blessed is the man who does not walk in the counsel of the wicked, Nor stand in the path of sinners, Nor sit in the seat of scoffers! But his delight is in the law of the LORD, And in His law he meditates day and night. He will be like a tree firmly planted by streams of water, Which yields its fruit in its season, And its leaf does not wither; And in whatever he does, he prospers."* (PSALM 1:1-3)

Lack of Discipline

One of the saddest testimonies of many people is when they were called upon by God to make a difference in a particular area, but because of a lack of discipline in some way, they couldn't or wouldn't help. Usually the culprits in the area of discipline are how we control our time, our body, and our emotions.

In regards to time, we need to consider what we invest in our personal relationships, what our eyes engage in, and our interests. Are we spending time with the right people at the right time, especially those in our marriage and family? Do we have control over what our eyes are looking at and taking in? Do we know how to look away and do we know how to focus on the right things? Also, we must make sure that we are controlling our interests and not allowing our interests to control us. Do we have disciplined control over our body—what we eat, what we wear, what we do with it? And what about over our emotions? Do we talk with others about things that bother us in order to process them, or hold them in until we explode? Do we allow ourselves to cry or laugh? Do we control our anger? An often-overlooked area regarding discipline of emotions involves working through the wounds and losses that we have endured in our lives. Jesus says that in this world we will be blessed if we learn the process of grieving. Have we allowed time for grieving past hurts?

> "My son, if you have become surety for your neighbor, Have given a pledge for a stranger, If you have been snared with the words of your mouth, Have been caught with the words of your mouth, Do this then, my son, and deliver yourself; Since you have come into the hand of your neighbor, Go, humble yourself, and importune your neighbor. Give no sleep to your eyes, Nor slumber to your eyelids; Deliver yourself like a gazelle from the hunter's hand And like a bird from the hand of the fowler. Go to the ant, O sluggard, Observe her ways and be wise, Which, having no chief, Officer or ruler, Prepares her food in the summer And gathers her provision in the harvest.

How long will you lie down, O sluggard? When will you arise from your sleep? "A little sleep, a little slumber, A little folding of the hands to rest"— Your poverty will come in like a vagabond And your need like an armed man." (PROVERBS 6:1-11)

Lack of Knowledge

One of the consistent things that holds people back from pursuing God with abandon is a lack of knowledge. This is why it is so crucial that you continue to take classes and read books like this one that will expand your understanding for making the decisions that are crucial for living a life in the will of God. What do we need to learn? What do we need to learn how to live as a Christian and how to think as a Christian? This means, of course, that we continue to explore how Jesus wants us to live in the major relationships of life. It also means that we continue to grow in our understanding of God, of people, of God's principles, and of the various other Christian truths that give us a more complete picture of this world.

"Grace and peace be multiplied to you in the knowledge of God and of Jesus our Lord; seeing that His divine power has granted to us everything pertaining to life and godliness, through the true knowledge of Him who called us by His own glory and excellence. For by these He has granted to us His precious and magnificent promises, so that by them you may become partakers of the divine nature, having escaped the corruption that is in the world by lust." (2 PETER 1:2-4)

"...but grow in the grace and knowledge of our Lord and Savior Jesus Christ. To Him be the glory, both now and to the day of eternity. Amen." (2 PETER 3:18)

"The proverbs of Solomon the son of David, king of Israel: To know wisdom and instruction, To discern the sayings of understanding, To receive instruction in wise behavior, Righteousness, justice and equity; To give prudence to the naive, To the youth knowledge and discretion, A wise man will hear and increase in learning, And a man of understanding will acquire wise counsel, To understand a proverb and a figure, The words of the wise and their riddles." (PROVERBS 1:1-6)

Lack of Faith

Saint Augustine said that faith is indirect knowledge and it is the key to life. We will have direct knowledge of very few things in this world. We must take the word of someone else or some book. What better person to put our faith in than God and His book called the Bible? Do not miss the exciting life God has for you because you are not willing to trust. Faith is what moves us forward. There are some journeys that we are meant to take and they will change our lives beyond what we could imagine.

"Now faith is the assurance of things hoped for, the conviction of things not seen. For by it the men of old gained approval. By faith we understand that the worlds were prepared by the word of God, so that what is seen was not made out of things which are visible. By faith Abel offered to God a better sacrifice than Cain, through

which he obtained the testimony that he was righteous, God testifying about his gifts, and through faith, though he is dead, he still speaks. By faith Enoch was taken up so that he would not see death; AND HE WAS NOT FOUND BECAUSE GOD TOOK HIM UP; *for he obtained the witness that before his being taken up he was pleasing to God.*

And without faith it is impossible to please Him, for he who comes to God must believe that He is and that He is a rewarder of those who seek Him. By faith Noah, being warned by God about things not yet seen, in reverence prepared an ark for the salvation of his household, by which he condemned the world, and became an heir of the righteousness which is according to faith.

By faith Abraham, when he was called, obeyed by going out to a place which he was to receive for an inheritance; and he went out, not knowing where he was going. By faith he lived as an alien in the land of promise, as in a foreign land, dwelling in tents with Isaac and Jacob, fellow heirs of the same promise; for he was looking for the city which has foundations, whose architect and builder is God. By faith even Sarah herself received ability to conceive, even beyond the proper time of life, since she considered Him faithful who had promised.

Therefore there was born even of one man, and him as good as dead at that, as many descendants AS THE STARS OF HEAVEN IN NUMBER, AND INNUMERABLE AS THE SAND WHICH IS BY THE SEASHORE. *All these died in faith, without receiving the promises, but having seen them and having welcomed them from a distance, and having confessed that they were strangers and exiles on the earth. For those who say such things make it clear that they are seeking a country of their own. And indeed if they had been thinking of that country from which they went out, they would have had opportunity to return. But as it is, they desire a better country, that is, a heavenly one. Therefore God is not ashamed to be called their God; for He has prepared a city for them."* (HEBREWS 11:1-40)

Conclusion

The will of God is not complicated, but it is not simplistic either. As we have come to understand, it involves making wise decisions, filling our relationships with love, and embracing how God wants to use us as a unique creation for others benefit and our joy. Enjoy God and live in His will. It is totally worth it. Remember that we will only be able to find satisfaction and fulfillment in our work and service to God as we:

1. Admit that God made each of us with a unique package of abilities.
2. Realize that God has a plan and program to maximally use us.
3. Discover and utilize who God made us to be.

Conclusion

This book and class has been about building a foundation under the Christian that will last through their lifetime. Christianity is not a sprint but a marathon of pursuing and pleasing God. In understanding Jesus and the Christian life, we have given you a much deeper look at who Jesus is and how by asking Him to take your sins, you will be given His perfection. We have suggested reasons why a person may pray a prayer of acceptance of Jesus and yet nothing happens.

As a follower of Christ, we have built under you by suggesting that you get baptized and begin learning how to live and think as a Christian. We suggested that you spend an hour a day interacting with God through the spiritual exercises embodied in C.H.R.I.S.T., which stands for Confession, Holy Spirit, Reading and Repetition, Interaction (Bible Study and Prayer), Service, and Thankfulness. We encouraged you to begin a lifelong process of learning how to let Jesus' principles run the ten major relationship of your life. We gave an overview of the ten spiritual realities that are crucial to thinking as a Christian and seeing the world realistically.

In building the foundation of a Christian, we helped you see the wonder of the church by pointing out the unique things that the church is supposed to do. While the church has not always been doing what Jesus commanded, the church, even if it is only doing close to what Jesus wants, is capable of amazing miracles in God's power. We saw that the church is supposed to model servant leadership, announce God's forgiveness, connect people of diverse backgrounds around the common core of God's forgiveness, grow people away from their natural selfishness and into a life of love and gentleness, raise up an army to attack the problems that evil and selfishness produce, develop a heartbeat of generosity in each Christian life, force people to see the transcendent and the hope in the world, look to reach out to people in love, and structure the church for maximum impact, not maximum control.

The final building block of a good foundation for the Christian life is to understand how to live in the will of God. We explored the three aspects of the will of God. First, we explored how to make a wise decision guided by the Holy Spirit. Second, we learned how to fill our lives with love and its fruits so that the richness of life will come through and flow out of us in priority order so the love does not become wasted or run out. Third, we came to understand how our unique gifts, passions, experiences, and opportunities have been baked into our lives and tell us where we need to help.

Building a foundation for our Christian lives is important and requires the time and attention that you will give it by working through this book. The sturdiness of the foundation determines the stability of the life that is built upon it. The decision to follow Christ is a good one and the decision to dig deep into the rock to lay a proper foundation is critical in the long run. God bless you as you continue to build a strong foundation in Christ.

"Therefore everyone who hears these words of Mine and acts on them, may be compared to a wise man who built his house on the rock. "And the rain fell, and the floods came, and the winds blew and slammed against that house; and yet it did not fall, for it had been founded on the rock. "Everyone who hears these words of Mine and does not act on them, will be like a foolish man who built his house on the sand. "The rain fell, and the floods came, and the winds blew and slammed against that house; and it fell—and great was its fall." When Jesus had finished these words, the crowds were amazed at His teaching; for He was teaching them as one having authority, and not as their scribes."

(MATT. 7:24-29)

Appendix 1
Answering the Ten Big Questions of Life from a Christian Worldview

Every philosophy or religion down through the history of time must ask and answer a number of basic questions in order to supply real answers to its followers. These questions and answers form the way that a philosophy or religion thinks and sees the world. This is their orthodoxy or their worldview. Christianity has a worldview. It has the best answers to these basic questions of life.

Christianity answers these questions with the truths that we call Christian doctrine. When we embrace these truths, our lives change because of them. Becoming a Christ follower means exploring, understanding, and believing the Christian answers to the basic questions of life. This will require some thinking, reading, and discussing as you move forward in your understanding of the Christian worldview. Let's put our thinking caps on and plunge forward. In each case, I have explained the Christian answer and have put verses of Scripture from which that answer has been derived. My hope is that you will look up each of these passages and study them for yourself.

What Are the Ten Basic Questions of Life?

1. What is the ultimate reality? (How did the world and the universe come to exist?)

2. Who or what is the true prophet of the correct knowledge?

3. What is/are the active agents in this world?

4. What is the sacred book that reveals the correct truths?

5. What is mankind? (Who am I? Why am I here?)

6. What is success? (Why is there evil? What is good?)

7. What institutions are required for a well-ordered society?

8. Are there other intelligent beings in this world other than humans?

9. What happens after a person dies?

10. What marks the end of history?

Comparison of Various Philosophies and Religions with Christianity

For the last thousand years in Western civilization we have largely answered these questions with Christian answers and we became so used to the answers that we just referred to them without asking the preceding questions. These answers are called Christian doctrine, the pillars of Christian truth, and the Christian understanding of the world. Other philosophies and religions also offer their answers to the basic questions of life, a few of which are highlighted in the chart below. Spend a few minutes and think about how the answers to these categories might affect someone's worldview and how their actions might be impacted or explained.

Category	Christianity	Islam	Naturalism	Buddhism
Ultimate Reality	God	Allah	Matter	Oneness
Prophet	Jesus	Mohammed	Charles Darwin	Buddha
Active Agent	Holy Spirit	Allah	Mutation & Natural Selection	The Oneness
Sacred Writing	The Bible	Koran	Origin of the Species	The Tripitaka, Sutras, Tibetan book of the dead
Why & What Is Man?	Man: Image Bearer of God/Sinful	The servant and/or slave of Allah	An evolutionary accident	Sufferer
What is Success?	Salvation: Loving God, Others & Self	Submission to Allah	Collecting Money, Sex, Power, Things	The 8-fold path; Nirvana
Promoter / Worldview Group	Church	Mosque	School System	Temple / Monastery
Other Beings	Angels	Angels	Aliens	Many Manifestations
After Life	Judgment Day; Heaven; Hell	Islamic Heaven or Hell	None	Karma and Reincarnation
End of History	The Return of Christ	Return of the 12th Imam	Super Nova	Absorption in the Oneness

1. What is the Ultimate Reality?
We understand and believe that it is God Almighty.

The Ultimate Reality is a transcendent, pure, Spirit being. He is the creator and originator of the Universe, mankind, and our world. He is above, beyond, and before all things. The vastness of who He is cannot fully be comprehended by humanity. He has chosen to reveal Himself in the stories and truths of the Bible. He is a pure spirit being without our usual physical markers of identification. He describes Himself through His essence, His attributes, His nature, His names, and His major works as explained in the Bible. The information contained in the Bible does not completely explain God but it is what humanity can fully comprehend about Him.

Action Step
Look up the following verses:
- Exodus 34:6,7
- Psalm 139:7-12
- Acts 17:24,25
- Exodus 3:13-15

2. Who is the prophet of the truth? We understand and believe that He is Jesus Christ.

Jesus is the second person within the one Almighty Triune God. He existed as the Divine Logos before He was born of the Virgin Mary as Jesus of Nazareth. His birth was the declaration that God loves the world and was risking His only begotten Son to redeem those who would believe in Him. God was not writing off this rebellious, sinful planet and its inhabitants; instead, He was investing in its redemption. The divine Son of God became a man so that He could live a perfect life and then willingly sacrifice that life to open a way back to God for a sinful, rebellious, and damaged humanity. He died on a cross as the sacrifice for the sins of mankind. He rose again from the dead to prove His victory over death. He ascended into Heaven and has sat down at the right hand of the Father where He prays for us in our spiritual journey.

Action Step
Look up the following verses:
- Isaiah 9:6
- Luke 1:31-33
- Revelation 1:17,18

3. Who or what is the active agent in the Universe? We understand and believe that He is the Holy Spirit.

The Holy Spirit is the third person of the one Almighty Transcendent God and one of, if not the primary, active agents in the world. He existed with God and is God from all eternity. He is a person not a force. This Hagious (completely pure and transcendent) Spirit has all the attributes and divinity of the other two Transcendent personalities. They all reside in one Transcendent Tri-personal Unity. The Hagios Spirit extends two kinds of gracious activity to our world. One is called common grace, which is for everyone, and the second is specific grace, which is for those who believe in and follow the Transcendent One. He has guided and ministered to believers down through the ages. Since Jesus' life, ministry, death, resurrection, and ascension, the Holy Spirit comes to be with and indwell believers. The Holy Spirit has many ministries that He performs for believers and non-believers. He seals, directs, gifts, sanctifies, regenerates believers, and He convicts, restrains, and judges non-believers.

Action Step

Look up the following verses:
- Acts 5:3-5
- Isaiah 11:2
- John 16:7-14

4. What is the sacred book? We understand and believe that it is the Bible.

This Transcendent Being has communicated accurately with humanity over thousands of years in many ways, but most significantly and directly through an infallible, inerrant, written communication in the collection of writings we call the Bible. The Bible does not contain all we would like to know, but it gives us an accurate record of all we need to know to live a successful life, reconnect with the Transcendent One, and be in Heaven in the next life after this one.

The Bible is not a book about God; it is the book from God. God authored it through the men He picked to write it. He breathed His own spirit and life into this collection of books we call the Bible. It has been supernaturally composed and supernaturally preserved. It was written by God's direction over 1,600 years by different people. It is internally consistent and non-contradictory. It is God's message to humanity about Himself, life, wisdom, and how to approach Him. God made sure that the Bible did not contain errors so we could rely upon it when it speaks. It proves itself to be from God by writing history in advance. The prophecies that have been given and then were fulfilled are the watermark of authenticity from God. The Bible consists of the 39 books of the Old Testament and the 27 books of the New Testament.

Action Step

Look up the following verses:
- 2 Timothy 3:16
- Psalm 19:7-11
- 1 Peter 1:20,21

5. Who or what is mankind or humanity? We declare that man is made in God's image and has become sinful. We call it creation and the Fall of Mankind.

This Transcendent Being explains that mankind is a crowning achievement of His creation activity, created as unique bearers of the Transcendent Being's image. He created this universe and our particular planet perfect but allowed the choices of certain beings to have real consequences into this universe (free will). The selfish and rebellious choices of certain spirit beings and certain human beings plunged those individuals, their progeny, and this planet into dysfunction and brokenness. This planet and its human relationships retain some aspects of its original perfect design, but it has become a place of selfishness, violence, and rebellion.

At present, since the great rebellion, all humanity is both good and evil. Because of the rebellion and selfishness of our first parents, we are now capable of great evil. Every man and woman is rebellious and selfish and thereby cut off from the direct loving contact with the Transcendent Being that we need. Because of the continuing rebellion, selfishness, and disconnect, no individual human can redeem themselves. If we are going to fulfill our purpose, it will require a reorientation away from pure selfishness and toward true love.

Action Step

Look up the following verses:

- Genesis 1 and 2
- Genesis 1:26,27
- Romans 3:10-18
- 1 Thessalonians 5:23

6. What is success? We call it entering into a loving relationship with God, which then spreads a truly loving relationship to all others in our life.

The Transcendent Being has explained that lasting success is relational—filling one's life with love and connection toward the Transcendent One, toward others, and toward self. His two greatest commands are to love Him with everything you have and others as you love yourself. The Transcendent One knows that due to rebellion and selfishness individuals are disconnected from Him, from each other, and even from themselves, so He has provided a way to reconnect with Him and begin loving Him, Others, and Self.

Humanity needs salvation because of an introduction of evil into the world of the good. Evil is a deprivation of the good, a twisting of that which was good. It came because of a choice of our first parents and every subsequent person. It was originally introduced into the world of the good through the internal corruption of a separate creation of the Transcendent One. Evil exists because of the twisting of the good done by the Transcendent One's creatures. He has acted to remedy the corrupt actions without negating the reality of their choices.

This reconnection and reorientation to a life filled with love is called salvation. It is explained and illuminated through twenty-seven different metaphors, illustrations, and/or components. This reconnection and reorientation to love involves the removal of the wreckage of the past and includes significant improvement in life here and now, and full realization of our uniqueness and abilities in a life following this life.

Salvation is the act of God whereby He invites the unworthy and incapable sinner to begin a loving relationship with Him through faith based upon the work that He did in the life, death, and resurrection of His Son Jesus Christ, and to learn how to love others at new levels and oneself in righteous ways.

The following is a prayer that can begin your life of faith in God.

> *Dear Heavenly Father,*
>
> *I come to you through the work of your only begotten Son, Jesus Christ. I admit that I am a sinner and have violated your rules and standards in my life. I need your gift of forgiveness in Jesus. I right now accept His payment for my sins.*
>
> *I ask Him to make me everything You want me to be. Thank You, Jesus, for dying on the cross for my sins. I believe in You as my only hope of heaven and eternal life.*
>
> *Amen*

Action Step

Look up the following verses:
- John 1:29
- Romans 3:21-27
- Romans 8:28-30
- Jeremiah 31:31-34

7. What institutions are essential for an ordered life? We declare that they are the family, the church, and the government.

The Transcendent One has declared that three institutions are essential for healthy individual lives: The family – a man and a woman and children; as the basic unit of society healthy families are essential for a well ordered life. The church – a community of individuals who believe and support a common worldview; The church is the creation of God to change the world by creating, providing for and releasing believers into this present sinful world to do God's work. The government – a ruling group of individuals who protect the individuals and order the society is essential. Each community needs a governmental structure to promote good behavior and restrict evil behavior.

Action Step
Look up the following verses:
- Matthew 16:16-19
- Ephesians 4:11-16
- Acts 2:41-47

8. Are there other intelligent beings in the universe? We understand that God has created other spirit beings called angels; some are good, and some have become evil.

There are other intelligent spirit beings that the Transcendent One has created to serve Him and assist humanity. There are at least 4 different kinds of pure spirit beings spoken of in the Scriptures. Some of these spirit beings have rebelled from the Transcendent Being's rule over them and are now humanities avowed enemies.

They seek to damage, obstruct and destroy human kind's return to relationship with the Transcendent One and becoming a reflection of His glory. Every believer is and will be tempted, disrupted and attacked to keep them from fulfilling their full role in the story of redemption.

Action Step

Look up the following verses:
- Hebrews 1:14
- Matthew 18:10
- Ephesians 6:10-12

9. What happens after death? We understand that after this life there are three significant places and/or events that make up the after life: Heaven, Hell, and Judgment Day.

There is an after-life that awaits all people. Consciousness does not end when our physical bodies stop functioning. There will be a judgment day for every person after they die. God will search through our lives to see what choices we have made. Those who choose to embrace God's gracious offer of forgiveness through believe in Jesus Christ's life, death, resurrection and ascension will be ushered into heaven where fullness of life will begin. Heaven will be a place of everlasting significance, meaning and intimacy with God. Those who choose to reject God's offer of forgiveness in Christ or those who seek to impress God with their own efforts will be judged for their sins and assigned to the place of weeping and gnashing of teeth. Hell is a monument to the selfishness of men and women who would rather be the captain of their own life in misery than the receiver of God's grace through submission.

Action Step

Look up the following verses:
- Revelation 20:11-15
- Daniel 12:2,3
- Revelation 21:1-27
- Revelation 22:1-10
- Luke 16:19-31
- 2 Thessalonians 1:9

10. How does the world end? We understand and believe that history, as we know it, will end with the return of Christ to this world.

The Divine logos came to the earth once as He was conceived by the Holy Spirit in the womb of the Virgin Mary. His first coming provided the crucial basis for the salvation that He offered. He is coming again to judge the world and to set up His righteous kingdom. The second coming of the Lord Jesus Christ will be spectacular and demonstrate that those who believe in Christ were right to put their trust in Him. He will end the misery and corruption of the present political systems and disputes. His second coming will begin with a shout and a trumpet when the bodies of the dead believers will rise first and then those who are alive will rise up to meet the Lord Jesus in the clouds. He will return ready for war and judgment. He came the first time as a meek and mild carpenter offering Himself as the payment for our sins, but the second time He will be a Warrior King.

Action Step

Look up the following verses:
- Matthew 24:29-31
- 1 Thessalonians 4:13-18
- Revelation 19:11-16

Appendix 2
Spiritual Gifts

There are over twenty different spiritual gifts. Once you become a Christian, you receive a spiritual gift from the Holy Spirit, which is to be used for the building up of the body of Christ.

PROPHECY: 1 Cor. 12:10,28; Rom. 12:6
The special ability to communicate God's truth with power and directness.

SERVICE: 2 Tim. 1:16-18; Rom. 12:7
The special ability to see and meet physical or tangible needs.

TEACHING: 1 Cor. 12:28; Rom. 12:7
The special ability to explain the truths of God in a clear manner.

EXHORTATION: 1 Cor. 12:1-11; Rom. 12:7-8
The special ability to challenge or motivate others toward a healthy relationship with Jesus Christ or alignment of actions with the truth of God.

GIVING: Rom. 12:8; 2 Cor. 9:2-8
The special ability to understand where God has resources and to put those who need the resources with those who have them.

LEADERSHIP: Rom. 12:8; Heb. 13:17; 1 Cor. 12:1-11
The special ability to set goals for the church and to move His people to accomplish them.

MERCY: Rom. 12:8; Acts 16:33-34
The special ability to see and alleviate the hurts of people.

WISDOM: 1 COR. 12:8,28
The special ability to apply the knowledge of God to a person's life.

KNOWLEDGE: 1 COR. 12:8
The special ability to discover and collect God's truth for use in the body of Christ.

FAITH: 1 COR. 12:9
The special ability to discern God's ultimate purposes and work and pray to that end.

HEALING: 1 COR. 12:9,28; ACTS 3:1-10
The special ability to see the hurts of people that God wants to correct and to be an agent of His grace on God's behalf.

MIRACLES: 1 COR. 12:10,28; ACTS 9:36-42
The special ability to discern what God would do in a given situation and to be the channel of His power and grace in that situation.

DISCERNING OF SPIRITS: 1 COR. 12:10; 1 JOHN 4:1-6
The special ability to know when demons are present, and the strongholds they claim.

TONGUES: 1 COR. 12:10,28; 1 COR. 14:13-19,26-28
The special ability to speak in another language (earthly or angelic) to the praise and glory of God.

INTERPRETATION OF TONGUES:
1 COR. 12:10,30; 1 COR. 14:13-19,26-28
The special ability to translate the praise of a person who is speaking in tongues.

APOSTLE AND /OR MISSIONARY:
1 COR. 9:19-23; ACTS 8:4
The special ability to exercise general authority over a church or churches, often with the ability to found numerous churches. Also, the special ability to communicate the message of the Gospel

in a culture different than your own.

HELPS: 1 COR. 12:28; ROM.12:7,18:1-2
The special ability to care for the personal needs of others in the body of Christ.

ADMINISTRATION: 1 COR. 12:28; ACTS 8:1-7; TITUS 1:5; 2 COR. 9:12
The special ability to implement, supervise, and accomplish God's goals.

EVANGELIST: EPH. 4:11-14; ACTS 8:5-6
The special ability to lead people to surrender to Jesus Christ.

PASTOR: EPH. 4:11-14; 1TIM. 3:1-7
The special ability to assume long-term responsibility for the spiritual welfare of a group of believers.

CELIBACY: 1 COR. 7:7,8; MATT 19:10-12
The special ability to remain single and enjoy it.

VOLUNTARY POVERTY: 1 COR. 13:1-3; ACTS 2:44-45
The special ability to materially live below the cultural nouns.

MARTYRDOM: 1 COR. 13:1-3
The special ability to undergo physical suffering and even death with a joyous or victorious attitude.

HOSPITALITY: 1 PET. 4:9; ROM. 12:9-13
The special ability to open their home and offer a wann welcome to strangers.

INTERCESSION: JAMES 5:14-16; 1 TIM. 2:1
The special ability to pray for extended periods of time for specific needs and to see frequent answers.

Appendix 3
Significant Questions Regarding Spiritual Gifts

What is a Spiritual Gift?

It is a gift of God's grace that allows a Christian to do a certain task with special effectiveness. (1 COR. 12:7)

Does God still give spiritual gifts?

God still gives spiritual gifts. He is the one who decides which ones, how much, where they are to be distributed. God will not cease giving spiritual gifts until Jesus Christ returns again. (1 COR. 13:10)

What are the general categories of spiritual gifts?

(1 COR. 12:4-6)

    a. There is the spiritual gift itself. This is decided by the Holy Spirit.

    b. There is the office or ministry where the spiritual gift is used. This aspect of the spiritual gift is distributed by the Lord Jesus Christ.

    c. There is the effect of the spiritual gift. This aspect of the spiritual gift is distributed by the God the Father.

Does each Christian get a spiritual gift?

Yes, every Christian receives at least one spiritual gift. (1 COR. 12:7)

Who decides what spiritual gift(s) we receive?

The Holy Spirit is the one who decides which special ability a Christian receives. (1 COR. 12:11)

Can a Christian have any gift they want?

No, a Christian does not get to request a particular gift. It is clearly stated that not everyone has a particular gift even if they want it. It is also clearly stated that we are to be submissive to the will of the Holy Spirit and put the gift He has given us into practice. The individual cannot select what gift they receive but people in the church can pray that God gives their church people who will exhibit certain gifts. (1 COR. 12:28-31)

Are some spiritual gifts more important than others ?

No, all are essential to the healthy functioning of the Church of Jesus Christ, which He calls His body. Some may seem more important because they are more up front. But each one is necessary and important. (1 COR. 12:12-27)

Are some spiritual gifts more profitable to the whole church?

While no gifts are more important to the functioning of the church, some are said to be more profitable to the whole church in certain settings. (1 COR. 14:5-6)

Is identifying and developing your spiritual gift(s) the most important thing that a Christian can do?

No, the most profitable thing that a Christian can do is to develop the fruit of the Holy Spirit: love, joy, peace, patience, kindness, goodness, meekness, faithfulness, and self-control. (1 COR. 13:1-13)

When do we receive our spiritual gift?

It is best to understand that the Christian receives their spiritual gift(s) when they receive the Holy Spirit. This is at the moment of salvation. (1 COR. 12:13) While some passages suggest that a Christian may receive gifts some time later than initial salvation, it is best to see these as special cases or as authorization to use the gift in the church in an authoritative way. (2 TIM. 1:6)

Appendix 4
Developing Our God-given Dream

You may or may not have discovered the dream or desire that is your specific "thing," but God will bring you in touch with it. It may be something you experience, or something you see, or something you hear, but somehow God will awaken within you the desire to do something in a particular way or in a particular area.

A key example of this desire is King David, who as a teenager was anointed as the next king of Israel. He had up to that time been tending his father's sheep, memorizing Scripture, writing praise songs to God, and killing lion and bears that threatened his flocks. Then God brought Samuel into his life quite unexpectedly and birthed the dream that would guide him the rest of his days. David had to wait for over 15 years for the dream to be realized. He was trained to be the king in the "school of hard knocks."

When *the* dream is first birthed in our heart, it is almost always misperceived or encrusted with all kinds of selfish desires and ideas. God usually has to strip those from our pursuit and show us the dream in a more refined sense. Moses thought he would personally be the deliverer of the children of Israel by murdering the Egyptians. King Saul thought that as king, his ideas for defeating the enemy were more important than God's orders. Paul thought that he would be the teacher who would explain to the Jews that Jesus was the Messiah.

Peter thought that whatever he said was from God and should be obeyed, even by Jesus! Abraham and Sarah thought that God would give them the son He promised through Hagar, because Sarah was too old. Joshua and Caleb thought they would lead their tribes to conquer the land of Canaan when they were 40, not 80! Jeraboam thought that God was setting him to be king, and that no matter what he wanted to do, it had God's blessing. John the Baptist thought that he would be the forerunner of the Messiah who would usher in the fullness of the Kingdom right at that time.

Each one of us has a God-given interest or passion, which drives us to accomplish a particular thing. It might involve some problem facing mankind; it might involve a particular type of people; it might involve the church, or it might not; it might be totally tied up in raising a family; it might involve a business venture; it might involve correcting some wrong or injustice; it might involve being an example; it might involve research; it might involve a presentation. There is a sense when you find it that you were born to do this. While this passion drives you, it also means specific things about the other areas of your life. They have to contribute to it and fit together with it. All that you are will be required to accomplish the dream that God has for you.

There are three general stages to the development of our God-given dream:

Stage 1   Pre-dream:

When we don't know what the dream or desire is...We must give ourselves to becoming all we can be in Christ. Serving Him in all types of ways and arenas, paying attention to what drives us, or whom God puts in our path.

Stage 2   Understanding and building the dream:

When we gain the education, wisdom, experience, and skills to accomplish the dream. We must remain faithful as we wait to be in the place we were made for. We get little glimpses of what it is like to be doing it.

Stage 3   Living the dream:

When you are involved in actually doing the thing you were called to do. Sometimes living the dream is only the first stage of an even bigger dream that God couldn't share before.

In each of the key relationships of our life, we have a God-given passion or desire. All these dreams come together into the larger thing God wants us to accomplish. The big dream is what we would like to accomplish for God. It is how we were made to glorify Him. It is what you believe God has called you to be in each area.

Appendix 5
Natural Abilities

The following list of innate abilities comes from the Johnson O'Connor Research Laboratories work on human potential. They have identified 19 abilities, which are discussed further in their book, *Your Natural Gifts*, by Margaret E. Broadley. They have also identified other innate attributes about a person such as eye dominance: an indicator of left or right-handedness; grip: an indicator of physical energy; taste: an indicator of your ability to taste a sour substance, and more. The following list is the innate abilities, which God has placed or withheld from a person and helps determine their God-given S.H.A.P.E.

Objective Personality:
The ability to enjoy and work best with and through others.

Subjective Personality:
The ability to enjoy and do best in specialized and individual work.

Graphoria:
Clerical ability, adeptness at paperwork and dealing with figures and symbols.

Ideaphoria:
Creative imagination, the fluency of ideas.

Structural Visualization:
The ability to think in three dimensions and to visualize solids.

Inductive Reasoning:
The ability to form logical conclusions from scattered facts.

Analytical Reasoning:
The ability to resolve an idea into its component parts.

Finger Dexterity:
The ability to manipulate fingers skillfully.

Tweezer Dexterity:
The ability to handle small tools easily.

Observation:
The ability to take careful notice.

Design Memory:
The ability to memorize designs readily.

Tonal Memory:
The ability to remember sounds, an ear for music.

Pitch Discrimination:
The ability to differentiate musical tones, a trait needed in playing a musical instrument whose pitch is not set.

Rhythmic Ability:
The ability to keep time, a trait needed to play drums.

Timbre Discrimination:

The ability to distinguish sounds of the same pitch and volume from each other.

Number Memory:

The ability to remember numbers of all kinds, to keep many things in your mind.

Proportional Appraisal:

The ability to discern harmonious proportions.

Silograms:

The ability to learn languages, or remember unfamiliar words, technical jargon.

Foresight:

The ability to look ahead, personal concern or prudence about the future.

Color Perception:

The ability to distinguish colors.

Appendix 6
A Small Sampling of Various Abilities

Please place a checkmark by those abilities that you think you might have. Then go back and write a sentence about when you used it or your interest in that area. One does not have to have professional talents in a particular area to have ability in that area. If you have done a particular thing and have abilities in that area no matter how small, then put that down.

Cooking:

Building:

Arts and Crafts:

Playing Music:

Singing Music:

Hand-eye Coordination:

Strong Muscles:

Endurance Muscles:

High Pain Tolerance:

Gardening:

High Speed Reading:

Careful Reading:

Abstract Understanding:

Practical Understanding:

Attention to Details:

Mental Ability with Numbers:

Sports (put down what type or types):

Artistic Abilities:
> Literature
> Music
> Painting
> Sculpture
> Architecture
> Design

Artistic Appreciation:
       Literature
       Music
       Painting
       Sculpture
       Architecture
       Design

Theological Understanding and Appreciation:

Spiritually Sensitive:

Research:

Problem Solving:

Inventive:

Creative:

Culturally Adaptive:

Ability to Travel:

Ability to Plan:
       Long range
       Short range

High awareness of justice, fairness, and equity:

About the Author

Dr. Gil Stieglitz is an author, speaker, catalyst, professor, and leadership consultant. He currently serves as Discipleship Pastor at Bayside Church, a dynamic multi-site church on the Northside of Sacramento, CA. He served for five years as Executive Pastor of Adventure Christian Church in Roseville, California. He is an adjunct professor at Western Seminary (Sacramento Campus), a church consultant for Thriving Churches International, and Founder and President of Principles to Live By, a non-profit discipleship and publishing organization. He is on the board at Courage Worldwide, a wonderful organization that rescues children forced into sexual slavery. He has been a denominational executive for thirteen years with the Evangelical Church of America. He was the senior pastor at a mid-sized church in Southern California for seventeen years.

To learn more about Gil, his books, resources, and teaching and consulting opportunities, visit www.ptlb.com.

Other Resources by Gil Stieglitz

BOOKS

Becoming a Godly Husband

Becoming Courageous

Breakfast with Solomon, Volumes 1 - 3

Breaking Satanic Bondage

Deep Happiness: The Eight Secrets

Delighting in God

Delighting in Jesus

Developing a Christian Worldview

God's Radical Plan for Wives

Going Deep In Prayer: Forty Days of In-Depth Prayer

Keeping Visitors

Leading a Thriving Ministry

Marital Intelligence

Mission Possible: Winning the Battle Over Temptation

Proverbs: A Devotional Commentary, Volumes 1 - 2

Satan and The Origin of Evil

Secrets of God's Armor

Spiritual Disciplines of a C.H.R.I.S.T.I.A.N

The Schemes of Satan

They Laughed When I Wrote Another Book About Prayer, Then They Read It

Touching the Face of God: Forty Days of Adoring God

Weapons of Righteousness Study Guides

Why There Has to Be a Hell

PODCASTS

Becoming a Godly Parent

Biblical Meditation: The Keys of Transformation

Deep Happiness: The Eight Secrets

Everyday Spiritual Warfare Series

God's Guide to Handling Money

Marital Intelligence: There are Only Five Problems
in Marriage

Intensive Spiritual Warfare Series

Spiritual War Surrounding Money

The Four Keys to a Great Family

The Ten Commandments

Thrive Conference:

Marital Intelligence: There are Only Five Problems
in Marriage

Raising Your Leadership Level: Double Your Impact

Spiritual Warfare: Using the Weapons of God to
Win Spiritual Battles

Weapons of Righteousness Series

If you would be interested in having Gil Stieglitz speak to your
group, you can contact him through the website
www.ptlb.com

CPSIA information can be obtained
at www.ICGtesting.com
Printed in the USA
BVHW091510220520
579925BV00014B/485